The Thief.

A Tale of Deception

By
Tim Sweetman

The thief's purpose is to steal and kill and destroy.

My purpose is to give them a rich and satisfying life.
John 10:10.

1. The thief on the cross.

2. Jesus talks to Nicodemus.

3. The return of the king.

4. The reason these things matter.

5. Heaven.

6. Hell.

7. Elijah, Enoch and Moses.

8. A rapture.

9. The tribulation.

10. A new Heaven and a new Earth.

11. The days of creation.

12. Church.

13. Baptism.

Foreword:

The understanding that we have of scripture has been passed to us by people who lived in a very different era to our own.

Our modern versions of the Bible, have been translated by theologians whose ideologies have been formed by the concepts that the translation of the King James Bible encouraged - a work that was completed over four hundred years ago by people who had their own slightly askew mindset, having lived in a period when powerful church systems and structures were all that existed in terms of religion, and were the only blueprint they had to relate their understanding of the scriptures to.

Spirit led revelation, with regards to scripture, has been in short supply.

Many preachers and teachers, Bible schools and seminaries, have continued to teach their students the same misunderstandings as those who went before, having little understanding, and even less experience of the kingdom that Jesus taught and came to earth to establish.

Modern translations of scripture have followed very similar lines of misunderstanding, the authors having been trained and taught in the same schools that follow

4

the rigid framework of beliefs that have been passed down for hundreds of years, from teacher to student.

There have been many divisions in the body of Christ caused by a misunderstanding of scripture and scriptures.

Denominations, schisms, cliques and separations do not give the Lord any pleasure.

In the age that we are now entering there is a hunger to have a better understanding and experience of the kingdom life that Jesus is inviting us to enjoy with Him, here on earth.

For a time is coming when people will no longer listen to sound and wholesome teaching.

They will follow their own desires and will look for teachers who will tell them whatever their itching ears want to hear.

They will reject the truth and chase after myths.
2 Timothy 4:3-4.

The thief on the cross.

There is no easy way to work into a book that challenges so much of the traditional Christian teaching that we have historically taken for granted.

And so without further preamble let us dig deeper into the scriptures. In doing so we may discover some uncomfortable, but life giving truths.

We will dive in at the deep end and hold our breath.

One of the most popular messages we hear today is the teaching that if we believe in Jesus we will go straight to Heaven when we die.

Despite the writings of Paul and others, which we will look at, this message is regularly taught from pulpits across the world and is backed up by the apparent fact that the penitent thief on the cross with Jesus went directly to paradise when he died.

So let us begin by looking at this first issue.

We can find details of the events surrounding Jesus' conversation with the thief in three of the gospels that tell of the life of Jesus:
Matt 27:38, Mark 15. 27 and Luke 23:32-43.

It is in Luke's history that we find more information, possibly because Luke expended considerable effort in collecting reliable personal data from various differing sources - people who were personal witnesses, in his effort to collate a true retelling of the events.

Two others, both criminals, were led out to be executed with him.

When they came to a place called The Skull, they nailed him to the cross.

And the criminals were also crucified—one on his right and one on his left.
Jesus said, "Father, forgive them, for they don't know what they are doing."
And the soldiers gambled for his clothes by throwing dice.
The crowd watched and the leaders scoffed. "He saved others," they said, "let him save himself if he is really God's Messiah, the Chosen One."
The soldiers mocked him, too, by offering him a drink of sour wine.
They called out to him, "If you are the King of the Jews, save yourself!"
A sign was fastened above him with these words: "This is the King of the Jews."

One of the criminals hanging beside him scoffed, "So you're the Messiah, are you? Prove it by saving yourself—and us, too, while you're at it!"

But the other criminal protested, "Don't you fear God even when you have been sentenced to die?

We deserve to die for our crimes, but this man hasn't done anything wrong."

Then he said, "Jesus, remember me when you come into your Kingdom."

And Jesus replied, "I assure you, today you will be with me in paradise."
Luke 23:32-43.

Matthew gives us a little extra information that we will find useful to bear in mind.

Even the revolutionaries (criminals) who were crucified with him ridiculed him in the same way.

At noon, darkness fell across the whole land until three o'clock.
Matthew 27:44-45.

On the one hand Matthew records that both criminals were deriding Jesus.

But Luke tells us that one of the criminals protested that Jesus was innocent.

Many have seized on this apparent discrepancy between Matthew and Luke's accounts as proof that the Bible can't be trusted, but let's look at these verses in order to obtain a better perspective.

Finding out why Matthew and Luke apparently disagree will also help us to understand the conversation that Jesus had with the penitent thief later, which, as we will discover, in its current reading makes no sense at all in any Bible translation.

If we dig a little bit deeper we will find that Matthew and Luke are describing the event of the crucifixion at different times during the day.

Matthew has recalled the situation when Jesus and the two criminals were first placed on the cross.

At that time both men were deriding Jesus.

He then tells us that there was darkness across the land for three hours.

Luke then takes up the story, after they had been on the cross for that period.

After three hours one of the criminals was still mocking Jesus, but the other, no doubt having heard what Jesus had to say to him, had realised who Jesus was and why He was being crucified.

One thief was repentant and had completely changed his understanding, which was revealed by his words.

The other thief still had no understanding, and in spite of his situation, continued to mock Jesus.

We can understand that in the intervening three hours, while they were on the cross, Jesus had spent time speaking to the thief, perhaps to both thieves, but only one had received a revelation of who He was.

Only one realised that Jesus had come to earth in order to defeat sin and death.

Only one understood Jesus' purpose there.

Only one of them had come to realise that Jesus was God.

He also understood that Jesus would be returning at some future time, to His kingdom.

We know that because he asked Jesus a question.

The thief had a request.

Luke recorded his request:

Then he said, "Jesus, remember me when you come into your Kingdom."

It may seem strange that there is a necessity to confirm what the thief had asked but if we are to understand the conversation we will find that it is.

The thief asked if Jesus would remember him when He (Jesus) returned to His kingdom.

According to our Bibles, Jesus replied to the thief:
"I assure you, today you will be with me in paradise."

The first thing we might notice, if we have been following, is that Jesus hasn't answered the thief's question.

The second thing is that Jesus gave the thief a promise He wouldn't be able to keep.

Wait! Hold on Jesus, you can't tell him that!

Why not?

The answer that Jesus gave can not be that the thief would join Him in paradise on that same day because Jesus would not be in paradise on that day, or for at least the next three days.

Jesus confirmed this when He told Mary outside the tomb, after His resurrection, that He hadn't yet returned to His Father.

"Don't cling to me," Jesus said, "for I haven't yet ascended to the Father.
John 20:17.

There is some debate as to where Jesus was during those next three days, but living in Heaven with His Father was definitely not one of the options.

In truth, it was forty days before Jesus returned to His Father.

So, was Jesus telling the thief an untruth?

And in telling the thief that he would be in paradise on that day, had Jesus misunderstood the fact that He was to be the first fruits from the dead?

Paul was sure that Jesus was the first to be resurrected:

But in fact, Christ has been raised from the dead. He is the first of a great harvest of all who have died.
1 Corinthians 15:20 NLT

How is it that this thief was going to get to sneak into paradise ahead of Jesus?

And why didn't Jesus answer the question that the thief asked?

The thief asked to be remembered when Jesus came into His kingdom.

The thief hadn't asked to be taken to Heaven.

According to our translators, Jesus gave a reply to a question the thief hadn't asked.

The thief hadn't asked to go to Heaven immediately because He had just been listening to Jesus talking about His future return to His kingdom.

So why would Jesus tell him that he would be in Heaven, with Him, on that day?

We will discover soon that Paul also wrote concerning the fact that the resurrection of the dead had not yet occured.

Surely Jesus was aware of that too?

So why would Jesus promise the thief that he would be with Him in paradise on that day?

There are at least three things in these verses that don't add up.

So let us try to unravel the mystery, piece by piece.

When we have done so we will find that the explanation is simple.

Just like a jigsaw puzzle, we have to understand where the pieces fit. If we get a few pieces in the wrong place the whole puzzle will look a mess.

To begin I will show you two sentences - you can decide for yourselves which one might be correct.

1. **Let's eat Grandma!**
2. **Let's eat, Grandma!**

The culprit that creates the difference between cannibalising Grandma and enjoying a simple family meal is punctuation.

When our scriptures were written there was no punctuation.

It didn't exist - it hadn't yet been invented, and so our translators of the scriptures, bless them, have had to guess where punctuation might be appropriate.

They have, overall, done a very good job in every way and considering the magnitude of the task, have been very successful.

There are occasions however, where their own understanding of the scripture has let us down badly and this is one of those examples.

Another thing to bear in mind in understanding the art of the translator is that the original text can not be transferred word by word, from one language to another, particularly into English.

Therefore the translators must put together complete phrases in order to give meaning to a sentence or conversation, and then transfer those phrases into the given language.

Keep in mind the question that the thief asked of Jesus and then look at the answer that Jesus gave after we have moved the punctuation by one word along the sentence.

Then he said, "Jesus, remember me when you come into your Kingdom."

And with our punctuation moved by one word we find that:

Jesus replied:
"I assure you today, you will be with me in paradise."

Jesus' reply to the thief is not *'you will be with me today, in paradise'*, but, *'I assure you today, you will be with me, (when I return), in paradise.*

We might find it difficult to understand why the translators have given an unusual rendering of a very common phrase that Jesus used every day, or why subsequent versions of the Bible have replicated their leading.

There are approximately ninety examples of Jesus using the phrase, 'I *can assure you today'*, in the gospels.

It was a manner of speech that Jesus regularly used when giving a firm confirmation of His words.

There are no less than two hundred and fifty examples of Jesus saying *'verily verily, i say unto you', as* the King James version has it, in the four gospels.

Which is the same, or similar phrase as, *'I tell you today'!* or *'I tell you now'!*

So, why our translators have used this one sentence to give Jesus an unaccountable change of expression we can only guess.

We can not exclude the work of our enemy within the text of the Bible. His schemes operate in devious ways, in the most unexpected places.

I believe it reflects the translator's own idea of what they had been taught, that occurs when we die.

Or perhaps there had been some pressure from the authorities, who were paying their wages.

Traditional beliefs, once established, are very difficult to shift.

Having restored the reply that Jesus gave to the thief, we can therefore, replace our pieces of the jigsaw puzzle in order to get a fresh understanding of the whole picture.

The three anomalies that we first wondered at, have disappeared with our new understanding.

Jesus didn't promise the thief that he would be with Him that day after all, but answered the question that the thief asked directly - *"I assure you today, you will be with me in paradise."*

The thief had become aware that Jesus would be returning to His kingdom, having had the conversation with Him during the previous three hours.

It was to this kingdom that the thief was requesting admittance.

The thief wasn't to be the first fruits, ahead of Jesus, and the resurrection of the dead has still not yet occurred.

Scripture often, if not always, gives confirmation of itself and we can find this conformation in not only one example but in two scriptures which we will look at.

We can find the first confirmation within the letters that Paul wrote to Timothy in answer to those who were claiming the resurrection had already occurred.:

This kind of talk spreads like cancer, as in the case of Hymenaeus and Philetus.

They have left the path of truth, claiming that the resurrection of the dead has already occurred; in this way, they have turned some people away from the faith.
2 Timothy 2:17-18.

Paul clearly had no illusion with regards to the resurrection of the dead.

He stated very clearly that it had not yet happened.

How then can some today declare that the thief was resurrected from the dead?

There were two culprits who, in Paul's time, were spreading false teaching that the resurrection had already occurred.

Hymenaeus and Philetus appear to have been the main protagonists, or, in this case, antagonists, who, along with Alexander, were excluded from the fellowship of other Christians by Paul, until they had learnt not to blaspheme.

Hymenaeus and Alexander are two examples. I threw them out and handed them over to Satan so they might learn not to blaspheme God.
1 Timothy 1:20.

This kind of talk spreads like cancer, as in the case of Hymenaeus and Philetus.

They have left the path of truth, claiming that the resurrection of the dead has already occurred; in this way, they have turned some people away from the faith. 2 Timothy 2:18.

Paul clearly took the false doctrine of an early resurrection very seriously indeed.

He was concerned that their teaching would spread like cancer, as indeed, sadly, it has.

There have been those who have been raised from the dead temporarily, as in the case of Lazarus, and many others, but not to eternity.

If we are not yet convinced, there is another scripture that will provide some light on the false doctrine of an early resurrection.

We can find this in the book of the Acts of the Apostles:

Peter was talking to the crowd after the Spirit had descended on the disciples at Pentecost.

"Dear brothers, think about this!
You can be sure that the patriarch David wasn't referring to himself, for he died and was buried, and his tomb is still here among us.

For David himself never ascended into Heaven, yet he said, 'The Lord said to my Lord, "Sit in the place of honour at my right hand
Acts of the Apostles 2:29,34.

Peter was sure that King David had not ascended to Heaven.

Had there been a resurrection of the dead to Heaven we too can be sure that King David would have been one of those who had been among them.

When we consider the seriousness that Paul placed upon the teaching of the false doctrine that the resurrection has already occurred, we might begin to give some thought as to how we speak to those who have lost their friends and relatives to death.

We often glibly announce that those departed have gone to be with Jesus in Heaven.

Let us consider the fate of Hymenaeus, Philetus and Alexander who also repeated those words.

But we will also discover, as we continue to place our jigsaw pieces in the correct positions, that our understanding of Heaven and our place in eternity has been seriously derailed by this one error, and the mass of false teaching that has grown up around it.

The picture that we have traditionally been presented with for hundreds of years, of Heaven, the kingdom that Jesus will inherit, our place in it and in eternity has been seriously corrupted by the manner that the pieces of the jigsaw have been jammed in the frame incorrectly in order to fit a theology that was created by man, for their own purpose.

As we continue with our discovery we might find that the completed picture takes on a very different form from the one that we have previously understood.

The return of the king.

I have written other books with regards to the kingdom that Jesus came to lead us into.

Some versions of the Bible refer to God's kingdom as paradise.

For a more detailed study take a look at my book, Entering Eternity Today.

For the purposes of this short exploration we will look at a few highlights that will further assist us to get a clearer perspective of our own place in God's eternity and indeed, whether we do have a place there.

The traditional starting point to get a peek into eternity is to look at the story of Nicodemus who came to Jesus secretly, at night, to ask about the kingdom that he had heard Jesus teaching about.

For such a well known story there are, again, many pieces of the jigsaw to remove, take a new look at, and replace correctly.

Our next story begins with another question.

We will begin with the question, what was Nicodemus asking Jesus?

When we understand that we can look at Jesus' reply.

Was Nicodemus concerned with Heaven?

And did Jesus explain to Nicodemus how to get into Heaven?

We will discover that the answers to both of these questions are not what we might have been taught.

Let's take a look:

There was a man named Nicodemus, a Jewish religious leader who was a Pharisee.
After dark one evening, he came to speak with Jesus.

"Rabbi," he said, "we all know that God has sent you to teach us.
Your miraculous signs are evidence that God is with you."

Jesus replied, "I tell you the truth, unless you are born again, you cannot see the Kingdom of God."

"What do you mean?" exclaimed Nicodemus. "How can an old man go back into his mother's womb and be born again?"

Jesus replied, "I assure you, no one can enter the Kingdom of God without being born of water and the

Spirit. Humans can reproduce only human life, but the Holy Spirit gives birth to spiritual life.

So don't be surprised when I say, 'You must be born again.' The wind blows wherever it wants.
Just as you can hear the wind but can't tell where it comes from or where it is going, so you can't explain how people are born of the Spirit."

"How are these things possible?" Nicodemus asked.

Jesus replied, "You are a respected Jewish teacher, and yet you don't understand these things? I assure you, we tell you what we know and have seen, and yet you won't believe our testimony.

But if you don't believe me when I tell you about earthly things, how can you possibly believe if I tell you about Heavenly things?

No one has ever gone to Heaven and returned.
But the Son of Man has come down from Heaven.

And as Moses lifted up the bronze snake on a pole in the wilderness, so the Son of Man must be lifted up, so that everyone who believes in him will have eternal life.

"For this is how God loved the world: He gave his one and only Son, so that everyone who believes in him will not perish but have eternal life.
John 3:1-16.

What we know for sure is that Nicodemus had seen or heard about the miracles that Jesus was performing.

He had put two and two together and come to the true conclusion that Jesus must have been sent from God.

He had further deduced that If Jesus had come from God, He must be able to answer his questions.

Nicodemus was a member of the Sanhedrin, he was used to hearing the views of religious leaders and debating what might be, and what might not be, without coming to any conclusions.

Now here was a man who actually knew the answers.

Jesus knew what was on the mind of Nicodemus and, according to our scripture, cut immediately to the point of his visit.

Jesus replied, "I tell you the truth, unless you are born again, you cannot see the Kingdom of God."

It was the kingdom of God that Nicodemus was enquiring about.

There is no indication that Nicodemus was enquiring about going to Heaven, or even about eternal life, although Jesus does introduce that aspect into the conversation later.

We have assumed that he was asking about going to Heaven because that is what we have been taught for hundreds of years but no, we find that Nicodemus was concerned about entering the kingdom that Jesus had been teaching about - these are not the same thing at all.

On one very notable occasion Jesus taught His disciples, and us, to pray in this way,

"May your Kingdom come soon. May your will be done on earth, as it is in Heaven.
Matthew 6:10.

It was God's kingdom on earth that Nicodemus was referring to, in his search for answers.

In truth, Jesus taught about nothing else but His kingdom on earth, and when we take a casual look through the gospels we can find many instances of this:

But he replied, "I must preach the Good News of the Kingdom of God in other towns, too, because that is why I was sent."
Luke 4:43.

Soon afterward Jesus began a tour of the nearby towns and villages, preaching and announcing the Good News about the Kingdom of God.
He took his twelve disciples with him,

Luke 8:1.

Jesus travelled through all the towns and villages of that area, teaching in the synagogues and announcing the Good News about the Kingdom.

And he healed every kind of disease and illness.
Matthew 9:35.

Heal the sick, and tell them, 'The Kingdom of God is near you now.'
Luke 10:9.

"Repent of your sins and turn to God, for the Kingdom of Heaven is near."
Matthew 3:2.

From then on Jesus began to preach, "Repent of your sins and turn to God, for the Kingdom of Heaven is near."
Matthew 4:17.

"The time promised by God has come at last!" he announced. "The Kingdom of God is near!
Repent of your sins and believe the Good News!"
Mark 1:15.

The word we have for '*near*' in this verse literally means within our grasp or, within our fingertips.

For hundreds of years we have been taught that there is a place in Heaven for us after we die, if we are born again, but this is only a part of the story - it isn't what Jesus taught and it isn't what Jesus told Nicodemus either.

Let us look into this conversation they had in John chapter three a little more thoroughly.

As we can see from the verses above, Jesus talked about the kingdom on earth being close, even within our grasp - at our fingertips.

He also taught several thousand people how to live within His kingdom on earth.

We only have to read Matthew's gospel, chapter five to appreciate the depth of teaching that Jesus spoke about living in His kingdom on earth, and that instance was only one of many occasions.

Nicodemus came wanting to know more about this kingdom, and Jesus explained to him how to enter.

Nicodemus didn't understand the explanation that Jesus gave at that time.

Jesus replied, "I tell you the truth, unless you are born again, you cannot see the Kingdom of God."

"What do you mean?" exclaimed Nicodemus. "How can an old man go back into his mother's womb and be born again?"

Jesus replied, "I assure you, no one can enter the Kingdom of God without being born of water and the Spirit.

Humans can reproduce only human life, but the Holy Spirit gives birth to spiritual life.

So don't be surprised when I say, 'You must be born again.' The wind blows wherever it wants.

Just as you can hear the wind but can't tell where it comes from or where it is going, so you can't explain how people are born of the Spirit."

Nicodemus was the first person, according to our scriptures, who had been told about being born again from water and God's Spirit and so we can excuse his confusion.

I have no doubt that he gained further understanding later.

But Jesus made it clear that He was not talking about Heaven, but about earthly things:

But if you don't believe me when I tell you about earthly things, how can you possibly believe if I tell you about Heavenly things?
John 3:12.

There can be no misunderstanding for us that Jesus was not telling Nicodemus how to enter Heaven after he had died, but how to enter His kingdom here on earth while he was alive.

The conversation was copied down by John afterwards, not so much for Nicodemus' sake, but for our benefit.

John had the experience of living with the indwelling of God's Spirit and so was able to understand the conversation better, later, when he had been reminded of it.

John appreciated that it is only through a realisation of our lost state, baptism in water and by God's Spirit dwelling with us that there can be a new birth.

It is the new birth that Jesus was talking to Nicodemus about.

We must be born again in order to enter God's kingdom.

But Jesus wasn't talking about Heaven, one day when we die.

He was describing entering God's kingdom life on earth now - becoming one with God the Father and Jesus in his lifetime.

Jesus talked a little more about becoming one with God, on earth at His last passover meal.

We can read about that conversation in John chapter fourteen.

When I am raised to life again, you will know that I am in my Father, and you are in me, and I am in you.

Jesus replied, "All who love me will do what I say. My Father will love them, and we will come and make our home with each of them.
John 14:20,23.

Jesus carried on the conversation with Nicodemus by giving him a picture of how eternal life would be accomplished.

No one has ever gone to Heaven and returned.
But the Son of Man has come down from Heaven.

And as Moses lifted up the bronze snake on a pole in the wilderness, so the Son of Man must be lifted up, so that everyone who believes in him will have eternal life.

"For this is how God loved the world: He gave his one and only Son, so that everyone who believes in him will not perish but have eternal life.
John 3:1716.

Nicodemus would have been very aware of the bronze snake that was placed on a pole that took away the sicknesses of the Israelites while they were in the wilderness.

Jesus used this image as a way of giving him an insight as to God's plan of healing for the world.

I'm sure that Nicodemus will have recalled this image and conversation when he saw Jesus on the cross.

Jesus told Nicodemus how to gain entry into His kingdom on earth, even though God's Spirit had not yet been given, Nicodemus would recall what had been spoken when the time came.

Jesus then linked the entry to His kingdom with eternal life.

When we are born again we enter His kingdom on earth and we also enter into eternal life - we don't need to wait until our old bodies die, but we obtain eternal life when we enter the kingdom - when we are born again.

It was Paul, when writing to the Galations, who said:

My old self has been crucified with Christ.

It is no longer I who live, but Christ lives in me.
So I live in this earthly body by trusting in the Son of
God, who loved me and gave himself for me.
Galatians 2:20.

If Christ lives in me, how can I die?

Can we now distinguish between going to Heaven when our bodies die and living in God's kingdom now, on earth, while we live?

There is a need for us to understand the differences between God's kingdom, eternal life and Heaven.

There are some similarities - areas that overlap.

There will come a time when these three become one - in truth that time is now upon us, but it is understanding them in separation that is important for us today.

We have talked about God's kingdom on earth - this is the inheritance of Jesus.

It is important for us to appreciate, if we are to enter God's kingdom, that there are two kingdoms.

By default those who are born into the world - that is everyone, live within the kingdom of satan which is a kingdom of death.

It is not until we come to a realisation of which kingdom we are living in, and our need for Jesus, that we can cross over into His kingdom - the kingdom of life.

We cannot live in both, with a foot in each kingdom and it was the experience of crossing over - being born again, that Jesus was explaining to Nicodemus.

Newbirth can only come about because Jesus died in order to bring us back into God's presence.

Eternal life is self explanatory - it is life that we live into eternity.

Some may also talk about the depth and quality of life that is involved but for our purposes we need to understand its eternal nature.

We can have eternal life because Jesus defeated death.

We no longer live in the kingdom of death if we have been born again - we have moved into the kingdom of life.

We might ask, if His kingdom is open for us now and we immediately receive eternal life when we are born again, where does Heaven come into the equation?

We will find out a lot about Heaven within these pages.

Heaven is the place where God lives.

It is a place that is often symbolised by clouds.

God led the Israelites in a cloud through the desert.

Jesus met God on a mountain covered in clouds.

Jesus entered clouds when He went back to His Father in Heaven.

The psalmist tells us that:

Dark clouds surround him. Righteousness and justice are the foundation of his throne.
Psalms 97:2.

Sing praises to God and to his name! Sing loud praises to him who rides the clouds.
His name is the Lord— rejoice in his presence!
Psalms 68:4.

The dwelling place of God is described as being, in the clouds.

The clouds describe His glory.

Righteousness and justice are the foundation of his throne.

The psalmist was not describing a physical throne but speaking about His authority.

The clouds are not where God physically lives but are a description of His glory.

It is pictorial language, placed there to give us an image of somewhere that God might be.

The scriptures tell us that God is Spirit - He is not visible, He is invisible.

No one has ever seen God. But the unique One, who is himself God, is near to the Father's heart. He has revealed God to us.
John 1:18.

We can therefore realise that God doesn't require clouds to live in - they are an illustration, given to us for a mental image.

Heaven is the spiritual realm that God inhabits.

It is a realm of righteousness - there is an absence of sin there.

Only the righteous may enter this realm where God dwells.

It is only because we have been given the righteousness of Jesus that He is able to dwell with us.

Remember the words of Jesus:

Jesus replied, "All who love me will do what I say. My Father will love them, and we will come and make our home with each of them.
John 14:20,23.

God has chosen to make His home, that is Heaven, with us.

Heaven is where God dwells - with us.

This can only be made possible by the indwelling of His Spirit.

Some refer to this as the baptism of the Spirit of God.

This is how Jesus described it to Nicodemus:

Jesus replied, "I assure you, no one can enter the Kingdom of God without being born of water and the Spirit.
John 3:5.

We have discovered that Jesus was telling Nicodemus that he could not enter His kingdom unless he was born again, through water and Spirit - by baptism in water and by the indwelling of God's Spirit.

Peter confirmed what Jesus was saying to Nicodemus shortly after the disciples were baptised in His Spirit at Pentecost:

"So let everyone in Israel know for certain that God has made this Jesus, whom you crucified, to be both Lord and Messiah!"

Peter's words pierced their hearts, and they said to him and to the other apostles, "Brothers, what should we do?"

Peter replied, "Each of you must repent of your sins and turn to God, and be baptised in the name of Jesus Christ for the forgiveness of your sins.

Then you will receive the gift of the Holy Spirit. This promise is to you, to your children, and to those far away—all who have been called by the Lord our God."
Acts of the Apostles 2:36-39.

We have learnt that God's kingdom is for us now, if we have been born again.

Our new birth is a birth into eternity - we need not worry about death again because we are born into a kingdom of life.

If we are born again we have God dwelling with us - Heaven is with us - it is a place that we can live in, if we are one with God.

We are invited to enter into God's dwelling place now.

Do we experience all that God has for us in the new kingdom, living with Him in Heaven now?

The answer to that question is probably, no, for most of us.

But because our immediate experience does not involve living in Heaven - perhaps we are not experiencing the indwelling of God' Spirit, this does not contradict the reality that Heaven - where God lives - is, in truth, with us.

If our deductions are correct - and the scriptures confirm that they are, why don't we experience living in that state now?

The answers to why we don't experience our expectation of Heaven today, can be many.

We can look at a few reasons:

One reason may be that our expectation of Heaven is misguided - our understanding is too often guided by the world - The images that come out of Hollywood, literature, television, newspapers.

Before the invention of modern media, folk lore, myths and legends gave the world misleading advice about Heaven.

The afterlife - what happens to us after the death of our bodies has been the source of much imagery and misconception since life began.

It was the Babylonians who initially gave us an image of many gods living a luxurious life that some earth dwellers might glimpse into.

The Greeks, Romans and other cultures continued with similar themes.

The image we have of Heaven, in our minds, is that of a place above the clouds somewhere - another place that is filled with good things - gold, silver and jewels - all of the things that man craves in the world.

It is the imagery of the world that has given us the idea that Heaven is somewhere else, perhaps high in the sky.

But the scriptures do not describe Heaven as the world describes it, in spite of what we have been taught historically.

The illustrations of Heaven that we enjoy reading about in scripture are exactly that - illustrations to describe a spiritual reality.

We might now understand a different reality, but we are still not experiencing what we might reasonably expect of a life in God's kingdom living with God.

Jesus said: *Seek the Kingdom of God above all else, and live righteously, and he will give you everything you need.*
Matthew 6:33.

Everything we need, sounds a bit more like Heaven doesn't it?

If we are immersed in His Spirit then Jesus will be all that we desire - we will be enthralled by Him.

His righteousness will be what our hearts seek - our only motivation will be to spend time with him - to hear His voice and to block out all other voices.

Are we in love with Jesus?

We will become what we devote ourselves to.

If our time is devoted to the world - our desires, that will be our outcome.

Do we seek the same reality that God seeks?

Or do we still seek the things that we formerly looked for before we were born again - before we moved into the kingdom of life?

Have our priorities changed - do our thoughts strain for the same things that God seeks?

Is our mind being renewed?
If we seek Heaven - the presence of God in our life, that will be our ambition - we will strain towards that goal and we will obtain that.

If not, the world - our old flesh - our desires and needs - our selfishness and all that involves, will become our experience on earth.

When that is the case, Heaven - God's kingdom - God's presence - the good things that pertain to Him, will be far from us.

If that is the situation we might wonder if we have entered God's kingdom at all.

The characteristics of Heaven are clear - they do not include all that we were told whilst we lived in the enemies kingdom.

Wealth and luxury may not be there, why would they?

Wealth and luxury tend to lead to a desire for more wealth and luxury, as does the thirst for power - there is no end to wanting more.

There is no need for wealth and luxury when we have all that we need - contentment is a far greater reward.

Living in God's presence is a reward that can't be measured.

If we have been touched by Jesus we will know this.

All of the ambitions that we strived for in satan's kingdom - riches, popularity, power etc. have no place where love exceeds all else.

Another reason we might not be experiencing Heaven could be explained by the manner in which we did, or did not, enter into His kingdom.

These can be many and varied.

Are we still carrying around with us the property of the kingdom of death?

Are the spiritual influences that we had there still living with us?

God will not share His glory with another.

"I am the Lord; that is my name! I will not give my glory to anyone else, nor share my praise with carved idols. Isaiah 42:8.

If there are demonic entities - things that oppose Jesus, still in residence in our life, we will not be able to enjoy the Heaven that God brings.

He is a jealous God and will not share us with another.

Ask Him to reveal anything that is coming between Him and all that He has for you.

He will do that by showing us the areas of our life that are not living in unity with Him.

It may be necessary to ask another Christian to help with this but often the Lord will simply show us what that might be and we will be able to walk away from it.

There is nothing else for us to rely on except the blood of Jesus.

He is pleased to give us the kingdom.

"So don't be afraid, little flock. For it gives your Father great happiness to give you the Kingdom. Luke 12:32.

We might try to enter the presence of God by a different means but we will fail.

It is only the blood of Jesus which has any power to open the door for us into the Holy Place with God.

In truth, the enemy no longer has any claim on our life; we are freed from his kingdom.

He will attempt to tell us otherwise but he is a liar and easily swept aside.

When we are baptised into His family we can leave everything of the enemies kingdom behind us - we can walk free into a new kingdom of life, but if we have not been made aware of that freedom we sometimes continue to live with many unwanted influences which continue to hamper our life.

If we are born again, the indwelling of God's Spirit will very soon make us aware of those influences that can not dwell in the same place as righteousness.

The baptism of God's Spirit is an amazing experience unlike anything we have previously known - living with Him will bring about change in us.

But this is not a once and for all experience.

God wants to be continually immersing us into Himself as we grow and mature.

There will always be new immersings as we move to different levels of the experience of living with God.

We have discovered that being born into God's kingdom is a journey that begins here on earth while we live, and continues after our old bodies wither and die.

Heaven will accompany our new life as we immerse ourselves deeper into God.

Heaven is a realm that we enter by becoming wrapped up - enthralled by Jesus.

God has called us to spend our time with Him.

And so, dear brothers and sisters, we can boldly enter Heaven's Most Holy Place because of the blood of Jesus.

By his death, Jesus opened a new and life-giving way through the curtain into the Most Holy Place.
Hebrews 10:19-20.

We will increasingly be dwelling in the Heavens of God if we immerse ourselves in Him.

The reality of Heaven on earth has not yet appeared for many of us, but that is a promise that is becoming closer as we learn to dwell in His presence.

Then that realm will become a greater reality than the realm of darkness - the realm of darkness is being overthrown now, as we learn to take on the righteousness that is Jesus and will continue to be overthrown as we all come to the unity that is Christ.

Paul wrote to the Christians at Ephesus about this:

This will continue until we all come to such unity in our faith and knowledge of God's Son that we will be mature in the Lord, measuring up to the full and complete standard of Christ.
Ephesians 4:13.

But we might ask how that kingdom experience manifests itself on earth and in our own life?

This will become clear in the manner in which we live with each other.

By relating in loving attitudes - by revealing Jesus to the world rather than our old nature.

When we begin to take on the righteousness of Jesus the world will see a different way of living.

The consequences of sin in the world, which affect mankind and all of creation, will be removed.

This is not the place to talk about how we as overcomers will carry out that mission or to delve deeper into the way that sin and death have impacted the earth and all that is in it, but we can know that all of those effects will be overturned as Jesus is revealed in us.

There is much work for us to do in the establishment of God's kingdom on earth - that is why we have God's Spirit dwelling within us - that is the reason we are here on earth.

It is for this reason that Jesus sent the Spirit to dwell with us.

There will be many events to encounter towards that end, but that is our goal and purpose.

At that time we will understand what John was referring to when he wrote in the book of Revelation:

Then the seventh angel blew his trumpet, and there were loud voices shouting in Heaven: "The world has now become the Kingdom of our Lord and of his Christ, and he will reign forever and ever."
Revelation 11. 15.

The reason these things matter.

For hundreds of years we have been taught that the gospel - the good news, is that we might go to Heaven when we die.

The truth is of far greater significance, and it is this truth that the enemy has kept from us, and aims to continue to keep us from entering into.

The good news that Jesus brought is that we are invited into His kingdom - into eternity and into oneness with Father, now - today.

Heaven is not an event that we must wait for, but it is a reality that we can enjoy now.

Jesus said on the cross, 'it is finished'.

When Jesus had tasted it, he said, "It is finished!" Then he bowed his head and gave up his spirit.
John 19:30 NLT.

Those words indicate that Jesus had completed all that was necessary in order to bring us into complete unity with Father.

But the enemy would like us to believe we must wait until we die.

By installing this deception in our mind he denies us the eternity that Jesus died for us to have, and also prevents us from overcoming him, today, in our own lives.

If we believe the false doctrine of Heaven when we die the enemy has won a major battle.

He prevents us from overturning the effect of sin in the world.

He also prevents the establishment of God's kingdom on the earth.

There are many Christians alive today who are not aware of the kingdom that they have, in theory, been born into.

These Christians believe that their only purpose on earth is to survive in relative harmony with God until they die and are then taken to Heaven.

This is such a sad misunderstanding of what Jesus came to earth to suffer and die for.

If this is what we believe, we have no purpose on earth except to hang on by our fingertips until death relieves us.

This is not the kingdom that Jesus died for us to inherit.

Neither is it the kingdom that we are called to establish on earth.

If we do not understand our purpose on earth or how we achieve that purpose, our lives are wasted and we will not inherit the rewards in eternity that we are promised.

We will not only miss out on the kingdom life that Jesus wants us to obtain and enjoy now, but we will also not learn to overcome the enemy during our lifetime, and consequently, we will not be invited into many of the rewards that Jesus wants us to inherit into eternity.

There are many rewards for those who are overcomers - those who are triumphant, or to use another word, victorious, during this life.

There will be little expectation of living a victorious life in the kingdom that God has presented to us if we are not aware of it.

There is a correlation between living in and establishing God's kingdom on earth.

In order to live in the kingdom we must first be aware of it, and to live in it and establish it in our lives, and on earth, we must know how to overcome the enemy who does not want us to enjoy the kingdom.

Satan does not want us to take the territory that he previously owned in our lives.

His aim is to keep us in darkness so that we won't achieve freedom from him.

And if we are not overcoming him we will certainly miss out.

The result of not overcoming him now will also have an effect on how we spend eternity.

If we are not overcoming the enemy during this life we will not receive fruit from the tree of life.

To everyone who is victorious I will give fruit from the tree of life in the paradise of God.
Revelation 2:7.

This does not necessarily mean we will not receive eternal life in some way, but each time we are triumphant we will add something to that life, both now and into eternity.

There is an abundance of fruit so why would we settle for one old grape when there is such a variety and plenitude being offered to us?

Whoever is victorious will not be harmed by the second death.
Revelation 2:11

If we are not overcoming the enemy during this life we will certainly be harmed by the second death - we will not be growing in maturity - we will not be ridding ourselves of our old sinful nature, which is the flesh, that Paul talked about, and neither will we be assisting those around us to enter the kingdom.

throw off your old sinful nature and your former way of life, which is corrupted by lust and deception.
Ephesians 4:22.

If we do not die to our old nature during this life then we will certainly be harmed by that old nature in eternity at the second death, when it must be removed from us.

Paul gave us a picture of our old nature being removed by fire.

But on the judgement day, fire will reveal what kind of work each builder has done. The fire will show if a person's work has any value.

If the work survives, that builder will receive a reward.

But if the work is burned up, the builder will suffer great loss. The builder will be saved, but like someone barely escaping through a wall of flames.
1 Corinthians 3:13-15.

If we are not overcoming during this life we will not receive the food or acknowledgement from the Lord that is vital for our existence.

To everyone who is victorious I will give some of the manna that has been hidden away in Heaven.

And I will give to each one a white stone, and on the stone will be engraved a new name that no one understands except the one who receives it.
Revelation 2:17.

Manna is the food that kept the Israelites alive during their wanderings in the wilderness.

The word, *'manna',* means, what is it?

The food that we can live by, day to day, is miraculous - what is it?

Jesus told His disciples that He too had food that they didn't know about.

But Jesus replied, "I have a kind of food you know nothing about."

Then Jesus explained: "My nourishment comes from doing the will of God, who sent me, and from finishing his work.
John 4:32,34.

For the Israelites it settled on the ground every morning for six days of the week and was a miraculous source of nourishment, necessary for their survival.

When we are victorious we also receive manna, in the form of words of life that sustain and empower us - they enable us to carry out the works that are already in place for us to do.

If we aren't receiving daily sustenance we can not overcome the enemy.

The white stone with a name on it that those who are victorious receive, represents the nature of the righteousness that Jesus has won for us.

A white stone indicates a state of innocence, whereas before we knew Jesus we were pronounced as guilty and our sentence was death.

Jesus has inscribed a name on that stone that only He and we know - it describes the battles that we have won, our new nature and the sufferings that we have experienced in His name.

It represents an intimacy with Him.

If we are not overcoming during this life we will not reign with Him.

To all who are victorious, who obey me to the very end,
To them I will give authority over all the nations.
They will rule the nations with an iron rod and smash
them like clay pots.

They will have the same authority I received from my
Father, and I will also give them the morning star!
Revelation 2:26-28 .

We are brought into the kingdom in order to grow - to become mature sons and daughters of God.

Our maturity involves taking responsibility in overcoming the enemy, who is satan - for making wise decisions - for overturning the consequences of sin - for opening prison doors for those who are living in slavery to sin in its various manifestations.

The degree that we are successful in that aim will govern the responsibility that we are given in reigning with Jesus.

We will be given authority over the nations, which will require some wisdom.

Jesus will rule as a shepherd - His staff will remove rebellion.

We must learn to follow His lead if we are to reign with Him.

The clay pots that are our old nature will be smashed when we are able to overcome the enemy.

We will be given the same authority that Jesus received from His Father, but only if we have learned to live in agreement with Father - only if we have learnt how to overcome the enemy who entices us to be prideful and self motivated.

The various organisations and individuals who oppose His reign will be brought into a place of submission.

Luke, when quoting the prophet Isaiah, described the opposition to Jesus as if they were mountains and hills:

The valleys will be filled, and the mountains and hills made level.
The curves will be straightened, and the rough places made smooth.

And then all people will see the salvation sent from God.'"
Luke 3:5-6.

The prophet Micah declared that the Lord's mountain is the highest:

In the last days, the mountain of the Lord's house will be the highest of all— the most important place on earth. It will be raised above the other hills, and people from all over the world will stream there to worship.

Micah 4:1.

We will also receive the 'morning star'.

The morning star is a description of Jesus who is the Spirit of prophecy.

Because of that experience, we have even greater confidence in the message proclaimed by the prophets.

You must pay close attention to what they wrote, for their words are like a lamp shining in a dark place—until the Day dawns, and Christ the Morning Star shines in your hearts.
2 Peter 1:19.

If we live in the victories that Jesus has presented to us we will receive him.

The spirit of prophecy gives us an understanding - a revelation of who He is.

He enables us to live in the reality of that revelation.

There is a far greater loss that we may encounter if we are not aware of the kingdom that Jesus invited Nicodemus to enter.

All who are victorious will be clothed in white.

I will never erase their names from the Book of Life, but I will announce before my Father and his angels that they are mine.
Revelation 3:5.

If we are not overcoming during this life - living in His kingdom, we will not receive the righteousness of Jesus.

If we are not overcoming, there is the possibility that we may be removed from the book of life.

If we are not overcoming, Jesus will not name us as His own, before His Father.

Can we begin to see how the enemy has drawn a mist over our eyes with regards to the need of entering into and of seeking God's kingdom during our life?

But there is more to learn about our need to grow in order to take on the responsibilities of the kingdom.

All who are victorious will become pillars in the Temple of my God, and they will never have to leave it.

And I will write on them the name of my God, and they will be citizens in the city of my God—the new Jerusalem that comes down from Heaven from my God.

And I will also write on them my new name.
Revelation 3:12.

If we are overcoming the enemy during this life, we will become pillars in God's temple.

God's temple is His dwelling place.

God's temple is where He lives, which is among those who are His children - His sons and daughters.

A pillar is in place to support the structure, which, in this case, is the body of Christ - all who have been born again into His kingdom.

Those who are victorious, support the ever growing structure by encouragement and by ministering to each other's needs - by removing the chains that the enemy attempts to bind us with.

We have talked about there not being a need for us to ever leave God's presence, which is also called Heaven - we are able to live in that presence in permanence.

If we are born again we are already residents of the New Jerusalem which emanates from Heaven - we do not need to wait for a time that is to come to experience the New Jerusalem - He is in our midst..

When we overcome we are given a new name that reflects our new character and relationship with Jesus.

If we are overcoming during this life we will sit with Jesus on the throne that His father has given.

*Those who are victorious will sit with me on my throne,
just as I was victorious and sat with my Father on his
throne.*
Revelation 3:21.

Through the Father's love we have been brought into
such an amazing place of undeserved honour and
privilege.

We are invited to be seated with Jesus on the throne.

The awesomeness of this invitation can not be
understated.

The enemy does not want anyone to be seated on that
throne.

This is why he spreads misinformation that causes so
many to be deceived.

We do not want to be included with those who are not
overcoming him, while we have the opportunity to do so.

Jesus is fully expecting us to succeed in the
opportunities that He has given us.

We have all the tools at our disposal to do so, and we
have Jesus.

The return of Jesus.

There have been many predictions and warnings with regards to the return of Jesus.

Historically the promise of His return has been used as a tool of fear in order to keep congregations and populations in check.

Many church goers, and others, commit to a life of compromise and hypocrisy as a result of the fear of being found to be living an imperfect life when Jesus returns.

The enemy has so corrupted the words of Jesus and His disciples that he has many enslaved to fear and insecurity as they worry about their own condition.

It is time for us to understand with a greater clarity the reality - the truth, of what Jesus was teaching with regards to His return.

We have looked at this event briefly already, but we must get a clearer understanding about the return, or perhaps we should say, the appearance of Jesus.

Matthew gives us some information from a conversation that Jesus had with His disciples:

Understand this:

If a homeowner knew exactly when a burglar was coming, he would keep watch and not permit his house to be broken into.

You also must be ready all the time, for the Son of Man will come when least expected.

"A faithful, sensible servant is one to whom the master can give the responsibility of managing his other household servants and feeding them.

If the master returns and finds that the servant has done a good job, there will be a reward. I tell you the truth, the master will put that servant in charge of all he owns.

But what if the servant is evil and thinks, 'My master won't be back for a while,' and he begins beating the other servants, partying, and getting drunk?

The master will return unannounced and unexpected, and he will cut the servant to pieces and assign him a place with the hypocrites.

In that place there will be weeping and gnashing of teeth.
Matthew 24:43-51.

Many have used these verses to teach that no one knows when Jesus will return - the event will come as a surprise that will happen suddenly to take everyone unaware.

But when we look a little closer into what Jesus was saying we can see that the opposite is true, Jesus was telling His disciples to be prepared and to be watchful.

Jesus told them that we must continue to be responsible and faithful whilst we wait for that time.

It isn't until Jesus gave an example of an unfaithful servant - one who abused his position and was behaving badly, that He talked about that type of person being caught unaware.

It is those who are unfaithful who will not comprehend the return of Jesus, and will be judged accordingly.

It is for this reason there will be great sadness, having missed out on the opportunity given to them.

It is from this verse that we first hear about weeping and gnashing of teeth.

This was a well used expression to describe extreme frustration and grief but Jesus wasn't applying the mystery of His return to those who know Him, He is warning us not to become unfaithful.

Paul also gives us an indication that the timing of His return will not be kept secret from us:

For you know quite well that the day of the Lord's return will come unexpectedly, like a thief in the night.

When people are saying, "Everything is peaceful and secure," then disaster will fall on them as suddenly as a pregnant woman's labour pains begin. And there will be no escape.

But you aren't in the dark about these things, dear brothers and sisters, and you won't be surprised when the day of the Lord comes like a thief.

For you are all children of the light and of the day; we don't belong to darkness and night.
1 Thessalonians 5:2-5.

If we are children of the light and day there will be no mystery of Jesus' return - we will not be surprised.

As to the manner of His return there is much for us to unravel - there are many pieces of the jigsaw that have been incorrectly placed in the picture which will need to be forcibly pulled out and replaced correctly, in order for us to see more clearly.

We obtain much of our understanding of the nature of the return of Jesus from the manner in which He returned to His Father.

And after He said these things, He was caught up as they looked on, and a cloud took Him up out of their sight.

While they were looking intently into the sky as He was going, two men in white clothing suddenly stood beside them, who said, "Men of Galilee, why do you stand looking into the sky?

This [same] Jesus, who has been taken up from you into Heaven, will return in just the same way as you have watched Him go into Heaven."
Acts 1:9-11.

When we begin to understand where the Heaven is that Jesus was taken to we can get an insight as to the manner in which He will return.

We have discovered that scripture uses the image of clouds as a way of describing the dwelling place of God.

As the disciples were straining their eyes in order to keep Jesus in view, we read that a cloud obscured their eyesight.

The disciples kept straining to see Him, but He had gone.

In our last verse we read that two men dressed in white robes appeared - we can call them angels, although the scriptures simply call them men.

The men ask the disciples, 'why are you looking up into the sky'?

There are many today who are still insistent on looking up into the sky in an expectation of the return of Jesus from that place.

But the men told the disciples that Jesus had been taken into Heaven and that He would return from Heaven.

The men told the disciples that, *'Jesus will return in just the same way as you have watched Him go into Heaven'.*

Despite what we may have been taught in Sunday school, we know that Heaven is not in the sky but it is the dwelling place of God, and that God dwells with us.

There are many scriptures that describe us as the dwelling place of God but we will look at Jesus' own words.

Jesus replied, "All who love me will do what I say. My Father will love them, and we will come and make our home with each of them.
John 14:23.

We can therefore understand why the men asked the disciples, 'why are you looking into the sky'?

The men told the disciples twice that Jesus hadn't disappeared into the sky, but had gone to Heaven.

The sky wasn't where Jesus had gone to and neither is it where He will return from, but He will return from where He lives with Father.

The appearance of Jesus again on the earth will be through His body which lives on earth.

Jesus will appear when He is revealed in us.

At this time Jesus isn't revealed in us on earth because the enemy who is satan has kept us in the dark about these things.

We have been deceived.

The pieces of the jigsaw are not in place.

However, when we begin to claim the territory that is ours and not his - when we begin to throw off the effect of sin that still clings to us from living within his kingdom, and when we put on the white robes of righteousness that are ours, then Jesus will be revealed to the world.

That time will be the time of the return of Jesus.

At that time He will be able to claim his kingdom.

Paul wrote about it in this way:

This will continue until we all come to such unity in our faith and knowledge of God's Son that we will be mature in the Lord, measuring up to the full and complete standard of Christ.
Ephesians 4:13.

Why do so many of us stand around looking into the sky?

There are some who claim that the return of the Lord must be imminent because the majority of the world has heard the gospel.

They take this opinion from a misunderstanding of a verse in Matthew's gospel:

And the Good News about the Kingdom will be preached throughout the whole world, so that all nations will hear it; and then the end will come.
Matthew 24:14.

There has been a general understanding that the good news is that Jesus died for us to go to Heaven one day after we die.

There is some distorted truth in this, but it is far from the full story.

It is this false doctrine that is being preached around the world.

There is a belief that when this doctrine has been preached throughout the world, the end will come.

However, as we have discovered, the good news is rather different to this, and Jesus tells us that it is the good news about the kingdom that will be preached.

There are few who are even aware of the kingdom today, and even fewer who know how to live in the kingdom in order to preach about it.

When the good news about the kingdom is displayed on earth (among us) - then the end of the rule of the enemy will come.

It is not, as some would advise, the end of the world that Jesus was describing, but the end of the rule of satan.

It will also be the end of the opportunity for those who don't know Jesus, to find Him.

It will be the end of the present era and the beginning of the rule of Jesus.

The scriptures give us an indication that the reign of Jesus will continue for one thousand years.

We may have a picture of Jesus seated on clouds, or seated on a throne, ruling with a heavy stick in order to keep everything in place.

Whether the number of one thousand years is a specific number of years or a symbolic number is open to conjecture - the answer is not relevant for our purposes.

We must bear in mind that the return and reign of Jesus on earth is with us - Jesus reigns with us - we are His body.

The reign on earth will be via His body, through the wisdom of those who have grown into a place of responsibility whilst they have had the opportunity to do so.

It will be a reign that is characterised by love - flowing from the Godhead through those who are intimate with Him.

Are we prepared?

Are we ready to reign with Jesus?

As we have seen there is much for us to do in order to prepare ourselves to see Jesus revealed.

We may be realising that rather than departing to Heaven when we die, in truth, Heaven is coming to earth.

Heaven.

We have discussed Heaven in some depth but it might be useful to reiterate what we know and to add some other helpful information.

The scriptures give us information about three Heavens.

The sky is described as the first Heaven.

The first Heaven is inclusive of the air we breathe and for twenty miles outwards until we reach the stratosphere.

We will need to remember this for when we get on to talking about a rapture, later.

The word we have translated as air, in our Bibles, is 'ouranos', the same Greek word that is elsewhere translated as Heaven.

Most modern translations have given us the word sky in order to bring some clarity, but the King James version often translates this word as Heaven.

And he [Elijah] prayed again, and the Heaven gave rain, and the earth produced fruit (James 5:18 KJV).

The stratosphere, where the sun, moon, stars and planets are, is known as the second Heaven.

And take heed, lest you lift up your eyes to Heaven, and when you see the sun, the moon, and the stars, all the host of Heaven, you feel driven to worship them and serve them, which the Lord your God has given to all the peoples under the whole Heaven as a heritage (Deuteronomy 4:19 KJV).

God's dwelling place is known as the third Heaven.

Paul wrote to the Corinthian Christians:

I was caught up to the third Heaven fourteen years ago. Whether I was in my body or out of my body, I don't know—only God knows.
2 Corinthians 12:2.

It is partly because of the manner in which the first two Heavens are presented to us, in order of distance, receding away from us, that we are inclined to jump to the conclusion that the third Heaven - the abode of God is even further away and must therefore, be beyond the stars.

Nothing could be further from the reality.

The scriptures describe Heaven as being in the clouds but we understand that this can only be a symbolic picture as the clouds in the sky could not support all that the scriptures tell us about the Heaven where God lives, if those things were other than symbolism.

God is Spirit and is invisible, therefore He needs no physical place to live in.

Christ is the visible image of the invisible God. He existed before anything was created and is supreme over all creation,
Colossians 1:15.

The visual images that we are given in the book of Revelation and elsewhere in scripture are there to give us an insight into the very real characteristics that accompany that which is involved in Heaven - in the place where God is.

The source of all life is God, who is love.

God presents Himself in various forms to us in the manner He chooses.

To Moses He appeared as a burning bush.

When the Lord saw Moses coming to take a closer look, God called to him from the middle of the bush, "Moses! Moses!" "Here I am!" Moses replied.
Exodus 3:4.

To the Israelites in the desert He appeared as both a cloud and a fire.

The Lord went ahead of them. He guided them during the day with a pillar of cloud, and he provided light at night with a pillar of fire.

This allowed them to travel by day or by night.
Exodus 13:21.

There are various forms that God has taken in order to reveal Himself to us throughout scripture.

To the Israelites, God chose to meet the high priest once each year within the holy of holy places, within the tabernacle, after the high priest had performed certain sacrifices and rites in order to go in.

We can appreciate however, that God was not limited by those situations and appearances.

Jacob was given a vision of a ladder, or staircase, that appeared to reach into Heaven.

There were angelic forms who were travelling up and down the staircase.

The stairway was an access into Heaven.

Jesus told us that He is the way - He is the door and He is the gate.

Jesus is the access to God - to Heaven.

Jesus told him, "I am the way, the truth, and the life. No one can come to the Father except through me.
John 14:6.

It is worth noting that it wasn't until Jesus departed to be with His Father, that God's Spirit could be sent to dwell with us.

Heaven - God, was not among us until after the Spirit of God came to dwell with us.

As we meditate upon these things we can begin to get an understanding that Heaven is not an inaccessible place somewhere far away - quite the contrary, Heaven is very accessible for us and extremely close indeed.

Heaven is a place that we are being invited into today, in the here and now.

Jesus is the access to Heaven.

Hell.

As with many aspects of the spiritual, it is the Babylonians and Greeks who have influenced much of how we understand the concept of Hell.

For them and for other cultures, both before them and since, Hell has been an alternative or counterbalance to their idea of Heaven - a place where those who were chosen, for a variety of reasons, could retire to.

The Heaven that was formerly understood by these cultures was created essentially as a place where the various gods who were worshipped by them, lived.

On the other hand, bad people faced a sentence of eternal damnation by being tortured, and in order for this to be the case, various myths have grown up around the gods who are supposed to rule over a mythical underworld.

The Greeks invented an underworld called *'tartarus'*, which was a place where the enemies of the gods were held captive and tortured.

Some cultures have suggested that it might be possible to either purchase, or earn, a safe passage for those in Hell and so to buy their way into Heaven - a place of eternal bliss.

It was believed that Heaven could be reached by carrying out virtuous acts or by being valiant and/or victorious in war.

The Catholic Pope's, and leaders of religious nation's, throughout the ages have endorsed the same ideas by granting forgiveness of sin to those who paid sums of money or achieved certain aims that were favourable to those in power - a forgiveness that was not within their power to give.

We have been finding out a little about the reality of Heaven from scripture - a Heaven that may be very different from the one that we have been encouraged to understand previously.

The Israelite nation had no concept of Hell, from what we can read, in their own teachings.

There is no mention of Hell in the Old Testament at all, but *'sheol'* is, which can be translated as a place of death, or quite simply, the grave.

The King James version of the Bible frequently translates the word, *'sheol'* as Hell, but this is not a correct translation.

There was no expectation in the Old Testament of a life after death or eternal life, let alone an eternity of burning in a place called Hell, but that life would be continued through their children.

There are numerous references to death and dying but *'sheol'* is invariably a place of finality with no future to be expected.

Isaiah foresaw a time when death would be no more:

He will swallow up death forever! The Sovereign Lord will wipe away all tears.

He will remove forever all insults and mockery against his land and people. The Lord has spoken!
Isaiah 25:8.

But it was Daniel and David who saw a day when the dead might awaken.

Many of those whose bodies lie dead and buried will rise up, some to everlasting life and some to shame and everlasting disgrace.
Daniel 12:2.

Some to everlasting life and some to shame and disgrace.

It is noticeable that those who Daniel refers to as being raised to shame and disgrace, are not also expected to receive eternal life or an eternity in Hell.

David states clearly that he has an expectation of being raised again at some time.

For you will not leave my soul among the dead or allow your holy one to rot in the grave.
Psalms 16:10.

Again there is no mention of Hell or a place of eternal torment.

There are several references in the Old Testament to a day or the day of the Lord, but these do not give any indication of an eternal torment either.

When Jesus arrived on earth, to teach about the new kingdom, Greek culture and Roman worship of the various gods, was at its peak.

It was to people who had been immersed into this culture that Jesus spoke.

It was from the traditional folklore of those who were listening that He gave illustrations.

Jesus often compared a life of sin to that of living on a rubbish dump, and the result of continually remaining in sin to be equivalent to being thrown on the same rubbish dump.

Jesus had a good illustration of a particular rubbish dump that all of Jerusalem were aware of.

On the outskirts of Jerusalem was such a dump which was kept burning in order to consume the refuse placed on it.

The refuse there included all of the general waste that we might expect from a busy town and also where the bodies of executed criminals, individuals who had been denied a proper burial, and dead animals would be dumped.

Sulphur (brimstone) was added to the piles of refuse in order to keep the fires burning.

This is where we get our reference to the fires of sulphur and brimstone that were continually burning.

It was a disgusting, smelly, site that was continually burning each and every day.

The site of the dump was in a steep ravine known as the Valley of Hinnom, which surrounded Jerusalem.

The Hebrew name of this area was *'ge hinnom'* and in the Greek, *'gehenna'*.

It is a place that is first mentioned in the Old Testament, as part of the border between the tribes of Judah and Benjamin (Joshua 15:8).

After the Baylonian exile in the sixth century B.C.E. it became the dump that was still in existence during the time of Jesus' ministry.

It is with reference to this smelly and disgusting rubbish dump that Jesus was comparing a life lived in sin.

So if your eye—even your good eye—causes you to lust, gouge it out and throw it away.

It is better for you to lose one part of your body than for your whole body to be thrown into hell. ('gehenna' - the rubbish dump).
Matthew 5:29.

The last word that appears in this verse is again incorrectly translated in our New International Version and should read *'gehenna'* - as is correctly translated in the Message Bible.

There are half a dozen other modern translations which have the word correctly translated as, *'gehenna'.*

The correct word is given in the original Greek script as *'gehenna'* and is listed as no.: 1067 in Strong's concordance of the Greek as, *'gehenna'* - *'ge hinnom,* in Hebrew.

Jesus was telling the crowds that for them to continue in sin would be like having their bodies thrown into the rubbish dump that they knew about - *'gehenna'* - the dump on the outskirts of Jerusalem.

Many translators of the scriptures have continued to support the incorrect translations given to us in the King James Bible.

This incorrect translation has continued throughout The New Testament in order to promote a false doctrine of eternal damnation.

As with all else, please research this translation for yourselves.

But, some might say, 'we are told that the Bible is the infallible word of God'.

Yes, that is correct - the original scriptures are.

It is our translators, who have given us a misrepresentation of what those scriptures mean.

Jesus and others often used a well known phrase of the time - there will be weeping and gnashing of teeth.

This is a phrase that has been used to reinforce the claim of a continual punishment, but in truth, this was a common manner of speech used at that time - a way of expressing severe anguish and anger.

"There will be weeping and gnashing of teeth, for you will see Abraham, Isaac, Jacob, and all the prophets in the Kingdom of God, but you will be thrown out.
Luke 13:28.

We find the same phrase repeated thirteen times throughout the Bible.

It is normally associated with the expression of grief that there will inevitably be when a person discovers that they have missed out on eternal life with Jesus.

But it is not a phrase that describes a continual suffering, but of a great sadness at one's loss.

The word Hell appears one hundred and sixty two times in our modern Bibles and yet theologians tell us that the word does not appear once in the original scriptures.

Jesus uses the term *'gehenna'* thirteen times and the word *'hades'* appears ten times in the New Testament; the correct translation of *'hades'* is simply death.

The two words, death and hades are often used jointly with each other in a given phrase.

The word, 'sheol', is used sixty five times in the Bible.

In truth the word and concept of Hell does not appear anywhere - not once, in the Bible apart from the instances where our translators have chosen to impart their own interpretation on scripture.

We hear some mention of hell-fire preachers, mostly from the deep south of the American continent.

Where did we first get the impression that those who do not know Jesus will burn in hell?

This idea comes partly from the Babylonian and Greek cultures - their ideas of Heaven and Hell, as we have discussed, and from a tradition of eternal punishment that was introduced by the Catholic church in order to keep the population in check by the use of fear.

The notion of death being a place of everlasting torture has been reinforced, by those who should know better, when repeating a parable that Jesus told, in Luke's gospel.

Jesus often taught by telling those around a fictional story, using relatable terms of reference, in order to bring a reality to what He was saying for those who were listening.

Jesus told a story about a rich man and a beggar.

These were both characters that could easily be identified everyday.

During the time of Jesus, being a beggar was a recognized trade. It was necessary to obtain a licence from the authorities in order to beg on the streets.

There were also very wealthy merchants, who the crowd would have easily recognised.

Let's look at this parable:

Jesus said, "There was a certain rich man who was splendidly clothed in purple and fine linen and who lived each day in luxury.
At his gate lay a poor man named Lazarus who was covered with sores.
As Lazarus lay there longing for scraps from the rich man's table, the dogs would come and lick his open sores.
"Finally, the poor man died and was carried by the angels to sit beside Abraham at the heavenly banquet.

The rich man also died and was buried, and he went to the place of the dead.

There, in torment, he saw Abraham in the far distance with Lazarus at his side.

"The rich man shouted, 'Father Abraham, have some pity! Send Lazarus over here to dip the tip of his finger in water and cool my tongue. I am in anguish in these flames.'
Luke 16:19–24.

We need to remember that this is a story that Jesus was telling, using themes that His audience would recognise.

The primary message that Jesus was giving was that of the vast and, impossible to bridge, void that exists between death and life - sin and righteousness.

He was also fulfilling the purpose that He came for - to teach about how to live in His kingdom on earth.

In the narrative that Jesus used, the rich man arrived in a place of death and the beggar arrived in a place that was euphemistically known at that time as, 'Abraham's bosom'.

Abraham's bosom was thought, at that time, to be the place where those who were righteous might go while they waited for the Messiah - the redeemer, to come.

We can appreciate that it is not possible for the dead to speak until the resurrection, but this is a story - an illustration.

The rich man found himself in a desperate place - death, with no opportunity left to alter his ways.

In the story, the rich man pleaded to be assisted in his situation.

The translators of the King James Bible have given us the word that Jesus used, - 'basanois', as torment, as have other modern translators since, following their particular train of thought, but the word can also be translated as pain and sickness, and also a place where demons inhabit.

The word, *'basanois'*, is also the word for basanite, which was a touch stone.

It was a 'proving stone' used to determine whether gold was pure or not.

When gold was rubbed on the basanite stone a particular mark was left to show purity or otherwise.

The place that the rich man found himself was a place where reality was proven or displayed - he found that he was not gold.

For the rich man, the reality was uncomfortable.

The phrase, 'weeping and gnashing of teeth', could also have been applied to his predicament.

The rich man, who was given no name - he could be identified as any one of us outside of the kingdom, asked Abraham to send Lazarus to relieve him, by dipping his finger in the water to soothe his pain.

It is clear that the rich man had not changed his way of thinking, he was still expecting to be waited on by

Lazarus, there was no humility in his new situation - no repentance.

But, in the story, Abraham pointed out that there was no way to bridge the void.

There is still a void between mankind and God with no way of bridging that vast gap, except through Jesus, who is the Way.

Whether the flames that the rich man was experiencing are literal flames of fire and were an indication of the hurt and pain that the second death will inflict on those who don't know Jesus, can be debated.

If that is so, this will be the only place in scripture where fire has been used in that context.

It is far more likely that Jesus was using the folklore that His audience was familiar with in order to provide them with an illustration.

If we would like to take a step deeper into the analogy that Jesus was using, we might come to the conclusion that these flames are similar to the flames that Paul used as an illustration of the fire that each of us must go through in order to be refined in the fire, producing a purity in us, but we must be careful how far we go with a simple story.

Historically, there has been some misapplication of the scriptures in the New Testament that talk about fire, which we will look at in order to bring some context to the symbolism of fire.

David spoke of the Lord's promises being like silver refined in a fire.

The Lord's promises are pure, like silver refined in a furnace, purified seven times over.
Psalms 12:6.

The more frequently that silver is placed in a refiner's fire the better it becomes as the impurities are burnt out of it.

One of the first uses of the word fire in the New Testament is in the words of John the baptist when responding to the crowds that came to him.

John answered their questions by saying, "I baptize you with water; but someone is coming soon who is greater than I am—so much greater that I'm not even worthy to be his slave and untie the straps of his sandals.

He will baptise you with the Holy Spirit and with fire.
Luke 3:16

What did John mean by this phrase?

A baptism of fire is a phrase that was used with regards to a soldier going into warfare and experiencing being under fire for the first time.

A baptism of fire was used by John to describe the difficulties that would be faced and overcome when we are born into the kingdom.

Fire is that element which either consumes or refines.

When we are baptised in water and Spirit we can never be consumed by anything as we belong to the Lord, but we will be refined by fire - the difficulties that we face and the trials that we live through will refine us - the impurities that we retain will be refined out of us.

Paul, taught about the fire of God that burns up the impurities that are our old flesh - the old man, is how Paul referred to our old nature.

It is our old flesh - that which is useless to us, that will be destroyed by fire.

The allusions to fire burning are normally, if not always, with respect to the removal of our old nature, or our sinful nature.

That which is not of God is useless to us and it is necessary, for our good, for it to be removed from us, and for that which is useless to be thrown into the fire.

John recorded a similar experience in the book of Revelation:

Then I saw an angel standing in the sun, shouting to the vultures flying high in the sky: "Come! Gather together for the great banquet God has prepared.

Come and eat the flesh of kings, generals, and strong warriors; of horses and their riders; and of all humanity, both free and slave, small and great."
Revelation 19:18.

John is giving us a picture of an immense ingathering of people who are coming into the kingdom.

It is a scene where the old worthless flesh of many is being removed and devoured, by the birds of the air.

We can be sure this is not a literal scene but a picture of the old nature being removed from those who are leaving the kingdom of death.

There will be a massive increase of people into the body of Christ in those days.

Our flesh is often referred to as our old selfish character.

We will not be able to enter into our inheritance with Jesus unless we rid ourselves of our old nature and take on God's nature.

These are the battles and the victories that we are to accomplish in order to gain the rewards that we will win.

We will discover more of these rewards as we continue our study.

The references to the burning of our old flesh has to do with ridding ourselves of all that the enemy attempts to put in our lives in order to keep us in slavery to him.

Paul wrote to the Christians at Corinth about building on no other foundation than that of Jesus:

Anyone who builds on that foundation may use a variety of materials—gold, silver, jewels, wood, hay, or straw. But on the judgement day, fire will reveal what kind of work each builder has done.

The fire will show if a person's work has any value. If the work survives, that builder will receive a reward.

But if the work is burned up, the builder will suffer great loss.
The builder will be saved, but like someone barely escaping through a wall of flames.
1 Corinthians 3:12-15.

We may build into the kingdom with gold, silver and with jewels.

These are materials that will last, they are compared with quality and the best that we are able to give - they are precious and will withstand the fire.

But if we build with wood, hay, or straw, these are worthless qualities and will be burned up.

Peter used the analogy of being refined by fire with regards to our trials.

These trials will show that your faith is genuine. It is being tested as fire tests and purifies gold—though your faith is far more precious than mere gold.

So when your faith remains strong through many trials, it will bring you much praise and glory and honour on the day when Jesus Christ is revealed to the whole world.
1 Peter 1:7.

Jesus advised the church in Laodicea to buy refined gold from him:

So I advise you to buy gold from me—gold that has been purified by fire.

Then you will be rich.
Revelation 3:18.

Peter referred to a future time when all of the evil in the world will be destroyed - removed, and uses the element of fire to describe that time.

On that day, he will set the heavens on fire, and the elements will melt away in the flames.
2 Peter 3:12.

The prophet Malachi spoke of the Lord being like a refining fire when He appeared.

"But who will be able to endure it when he comes?
Who will be able to stand and face him when he appears?

For he will be like a blazing fire that refines metal, or like a strong soap that bleaches clothes.

He will sit like a refiner of silver, burning away the dross.

He will purify the Levites, refining them like gold and silver, so that they may once again offer acceptable sacrifices to the Lord.
Malachi 3:2-3.

Malachi was expecting a fire that refines rather than consumes, when the Lord is revealed.

The Levites that Malachi referred to were the priests to the Israelite nation.

But Malachi was speaking about us, who are made priests.

He has made us a Kingdom of priests for God his Father. All glory and power to him forever and ever! Amen.
Revelation 1:6.

But you are not like that, for you are a chosen people. You are royal priests, a holy nation, God's very own possession. As a result, you can show others the goodness of God, for he called you out of the darkness into his wonderful light.
1 Peter 2:9.

At the end of a millennial reign of Jesus, John was told that sin and death would be thrown into a lake of fire - they would be disposed of.

Then death and the grave were thrown into the lake of fire.
This lake of fire is the second death.

And anyone whose name was not found recorded in the Book of Life was thrown into the lake of fire.
Revelation 20:14-15.

The writer to the Hebrews gave us this information:

And just as each person is destined to die once and after that comes judgement,
Hebrews 9:27.

Unless our old flesh - our old nature, is removed from us whilst we have the opportunity to do so, it will cause us grief at the time of judgement, or the second death.

Whoever is victorious will not be harmed by the second death.
Revelation 2:11.

So what of this second death?

Is this a time that those who don't know Jesus will be thrown into everlasting punishment - to be tortured - to be roasted in Hell?

The use of fire in scripture is normally indicative of refining or complete destruction, as in the case of the towns of Sodom and Gomorrah, or a time of refining as in Paul's letter with regards to a refining fire.

There is no indication in scripture of fire being used to torture or prolong a persons agony.

In the book of Isaiah we can read that the dead simply do not rise again - they will experience an eternal death.

The [wicked] dead will not live [again], the spirits of the dead will not rise and return; Therefore You have punished and destroyed them, And You have wiped out every memory of them [every trace of them].
Isaiah 26:14 AMP.

Hell has historically been used as a tool of fear and manipulation by powerful religious bodies.

When there is little sign of God's love in the land, satan rules over the lives of the population unchecked.

Where there has been a need to control or manipulate a population, the fear of Hell for those who do not tow the line has been a very useful tool to use, and is still used to keep congregations in place today.

There is often a fear of Hell in store for those who do not go along with the church rules and doctrines.

Where a church member fails to turn up for a weekly service there are generally mutterings about the road to Hell.

The enemy loves to keep God's sons and daughters living in a state of fear - a state that is far from the love - far from the freedom that is a characteristic of living in God's kingdom.

We do not need a fear to drive us into God, but we rush towards His outstretched arms of love.

With regards to the city that comes from Heaven, when the bride and Groom are united, we are told.

Nothing evil will be allowed to enter, nor anyone who practises shameful idolatry and dishonesty—but only those whose names are written in the Lamb's Book of Life.
Rev. 21:27.

There is no place to be found in the city for those who don't know Jesus.

We are told that there will be great sadness for them.

"There will be weeping and gnashing of teeth, for you will see Abraham, Isaac, Jacob, and all the prophets in the Kingdom of God, but you will be thrown out.
Luke 13:28.

Weeping and gnashing of teeth do not indicate eternal pain but a great anger and sadness.

There will be many who thought they would be included within that city but aren't:

"Not everyone who calls out to me, 'Lord! Lord!' will enter the Kingdom of Heaven.

Only those who actually do the will of my Father in heaven will enter.

On judgement day many will say to me, 'Lord! Lord! We prophesied in your name and cast out demons in your name and performed many miracles in your name.'

But I will reply, 'I never knew you. Get away from me, you who break God's laws.'
Matthew 7:21-23.

Jesus was saying two things here:

He was firstly saying that only those who do the will of Father will enter the kingdom (*on earth*).

Then He continued by saying that only those who do the Father's will in the kingdom *(on earth)*, will be recognized on the day when we are judged.

There will be very much anger and weeping when we realise how we have been deceived into losing out, and we head into a lost eternity.

Our redemption can only come through Jesus.

Enoch, Elijah and Moses.

We have discovered in our first chapter that, contrary to what we might have been taught, the thief, who died on the cross with Jesus, is not in Heaven.

There are two other notables who, it is often claimed, are walking around in Heaven with Jesus.

These are Enoch and Elijah.

So we will take a look at these claims now.

Have Enoch and Elijah been raised from the dead, contrary to all that Paul wrote about the resurrection of the dead having not yet occured, and contrary to what we know about Jesus being the first fruits raised from the dead?

Preachers often use Enoch as being an example of those who are alive in Heaven because there has been a basic misunderstanding of the nature of Heaven.

All the information we have with regards to Enoch is a few short sentences in the Bible.

After the birth of Methuselah, Enoch lived in close fellowship with God for another 300 years, and he had other sons and daughters.

Enoch lived 365 years walking in close fellowship with God. Then one day he disappeared, because God took him.
Genesis 5:22-24.

We must take some time to analyse what we know of his life and passing because what we believe of Enoch will affect our understanding of Heaven, eternal life, the kingdom of God, and our own foundation of faith.

The writer to the Hebrews, when talking about people of faith, tells us that.

'It was by faith that Enoch was taken up to Heaven without dying - "he disappeared, because God took him." For before he was taken up, he was known as a person who pleased God'.
Hebrews 11:5.

The same writer to the Hebrews used a similar idea when describing king Melchizedec, who met Abraham after a mighty battle.

Because there are no details of king Mechizedek's birth or death in scripture, the writer used Melchizedek in a symbolic way, as a man who *'lived forever'.*
Hebrews. 7:13-17.

It is likely that in the same manner, the writer to the Hebrews took the verse that we have in Genesis, with regards to Enoch *'not being found',* and expanded it to use Enoch as an example of the reward for *'living in faith'* and declared that *'he was taken to Heaven'*.

I do not say that Enoch didn't spend much time in God's presence in Heaven, as many others have whilst still alive.

The question is rather, was Enoch taken to Heaven after he died?

The writer of the letter to the Hebrews declaration is not found elsewhere in scripture, although Enoch is mentioned in Luke's genealogy, and by Jude, who talked about Enoch as being a prophet.

We know from our verse in Genesis chapter five that Enoch was a righteous man and he walked with God.

The only other things that we know for sure is that he couldn't be found, and that God took him.

The fact that Enoch disappeared and couldn't be found implies that people were looking for him.

There is another incident where a person was taken up into the sky and couldn't be found, although many people looked for him.

This was when the prophet Elijah, was taken up into the sky, by a fiery chariot, at the end of his ministry. *2 Kings. 2:11.*

He had just handed over his cloak of ministry to Elisha, who was to come after him, and all those around saw him taken into the air in that manner.

Elisha told the people around not to go looking for him, but they did anyway, in case he had been dropped on a nearby mountain, but they couldn't find him.

The prophets, who were his students, clearly had no thought that he had been taken to Heaven.

It has often been assumed that he too was taken into Heaven, but when we study scripture further we find that ten years after this incident, while he was still ministering on earth, he wrote a letter to king Jehoram. *2 Chronicles 21:12.*

It is doubtful that Elijah wrote that letter from Heaven, but that he was still alive on earth - God had taken him to a place where Elisha, who came after him, would not be overshadowed by the presence of his former master.

The death of Moses is another incident that involved a supernatural burial, similar to that of Enoch's.

Moses misrepresented God when leading the Israelites through the desert and as a consequence, although he was a man who walked with God, he was not allowed to enter the land that the Israelites inherited, but was allowed to stand on the top of a mountain to view it from outside.

Afterwards God took him and buried him on Mount Nebo.

There were no humans at the burial of Moses.

The place was kept secret, possibly because God didn't want his place of death to become a shrine, as had the cave of Machpelah where Abraham and his family were buried and the tomb where Rachael, Jacob's wife, was buried.

There has never been another prophet in Israel like Moses, whom the Lord knew face to face.
Deuteronomy 34:10.

Both of these men walked with God, as we have read that Enoch did, and after they were taken away by God, they were not to be found.

Only God and the angels knew where they were.

We have no knowledge of the burial place of either Moses or Elijah.

In the same way as in the passing of Enoch, they were not found, because God took them.

Enoch was a righteous man - a prophet, who walked with God.

There are many books, parchments, that bear his name.

His life was extremely short, until his disappearance, in comparison to those who went before and came after.

He lived just three hundred and sixty five years, that we know about.

If he was taken into Heaven, he may be the only one, I will not argue the point, but scripture doesn't tell us that.

It is difficult to make precise and definitive judgments upon a text that existed several thousand years ago and was written in a language, about which very little is known.

The manner of his early departure may be noteworthy, there may be another story that surrounds it, of which we are not aware, but we are not given any details apart from the symbolic writing of the author of the letter to the Hebrews, who also used the symbolism that Melchizedec lived forever.

But even within the symbolism of Melchizedek we know that he didn't literally live forever.

Enoch was a righteous man - he was a prophet, who no doubt spent much time walking with God in the heavenlies.

It is possible, and even likely, that his place of burial was concealed, as Moses' place of burial was, by God.

It is also likely that God transported him to another place, as was the case with Elijah, perhaps because he was being persecuted for his faith in God, perhaps because the Lord had a purpose for him elsewhere.

We simply do not know.

I have heard many preachers talk about the fact that there are two men in Heaven as well as Jesus - Elijah and Enoch.

Whilst this might be the case, it is unlikely.

I don't see any reason why they would be with God in that way, I have found no evidence in scripture to support that they are, and much evidence to suggest that they are not.

There have been many who have been raised from the dead only to die again, but in truth, Paul made it very clear that there are none besides Jesus who have been raised to eternity.

He wrote to the Corinthians about this very issue:

But in fact, Christ has been raised from the dead. He is the first of a great harvest of all who have died.

But there is an order to this resurrection:

Christ was raised as the first of the harvest; then all who belong to Christ will be raised when he comes back.
1 Corinthians 15:20, 23.

Paul said that all who belong to Christ will be raised when He comes back.

There can be no arguing with Paul's all - that means everyone.

If Christ was the first fruit of the harvest, as Paul tells us that He was, how can there be others who have gone before?

In fact Paul goes further and declares that *'all who belong to Christ will be raised when He comes back'*.

What we understand of Heaven has an impact on what expectations we have with regards to our responsibility and rewards in building God's kingdom and the return of Jesus to reign on earth.

Paul realised that none of those who had died would have gone to Heaven because he wrote to Timothy about the same problem:

This kind of talk spreads like cancer, as in the case of Hymenaeus and Philetus.

They have left the path of truth, claiming that the resurrection of the dead has already occurred; in this way, they have turned some people away from the faith.
2 Timothy 2:17-18.

Had Paul believed that anyone had already gone to Heaven when they died he would not have told Timothy to beware of those who teach such things.

We can conclude that the resurrection of the dead had not occurred during Paul's time and it has not occurred since.

Peter also, one of Jesus' closest disciples, said of king David:

For David himself never ascended into Heaven, yet he said, 'The Lord said to my Lord, "Sit in the place of honour at my right hand
Acts of the Apostles 2:34.

Had Peter believed in a resurrection to Heaven he would be sure to believe that king David had been one of those who had gone.

We too can be sure that, despite what popular folklore dictates, our loved ones are not looking down on us from Heaven and, as Paul confirmed, *'neither are any yet resurrected'*.

We must wait for the revealing of Jesus.

A rapture.

Having discovered that Jesus will be returning to claim His kingdom on earth, we might be in some confusion as to where the doctrine of a rapture enters into the equation.

If Jesus is returning to His kingdom why would there be a mass evacuation from earth of all the Christians who live here?

The truth is that there is no doctrine of a rapture - it is nowhere to be found in scripture, but is a fictitious event that has been manufactured by man.

Our previous chapters have explained the improbability of such an event and there is no explanation in scripture as to the necessity for it.

Our question as to why Jesus would remove the Christian community from a kingdom that He is returning to reign over, answers itself.

We will look at the origins of this false doctrine and why it has become so attractive and acceptable.

The doctrine of a rapture is often linked to a period of fierce tribulation that will be brought to an abrupt halt when Christians are taken to Heaven.

Both the tribulation and a summary wrath of God at the end of days are misguided and therefore there is no requirement to be afraid or to expect a rapture in order to save us from them.

Jesus warned that these trials would come but that we need not be concerned about them because He has overcome the world.

I have told you all this so that you may have peace in me. Here on earth you will have many trials and sorrows. But take heart, because I have overcome the world."
John 16:33.

From what we now know of Heaven one might wonder where these Christians expect to be transported to when they are raptured?

The mischievous nature of the insertion of this false doctrine has led to much confusion and many to interpret various differing scenarios as to when this rapture might occur.

There are four popular views on when a rapture might occur but the two main antagonists are the premillennialists and the postmillennialists.

Premillennialism and postmillennialism describe the views as to whether the rapture will occur before the reign of Jesus on earth or after, there are also some who claim we will be removed from earth during His reign.

But let us look at where this doctrine came from.

A rapture of Christians is nowhere to be found in scripture and neither is the idea alluded to in the Bible.

The idea of a rapture was discussed by theologians for many years after the scriptures became more available and popularly read, but it was an Irish gentleman by the name of John Nelson Darby who introduced the theory to wider Christian communities.

John Nelson Darby was born at the turn of the century - 1800 and lived until 1882.

He was one of the influential figures who founded the religious sect known as the Plymouth brethren.

The doctrine with regards to a rapture of God's children is a very similar misunderstanding of scripture to that of departing to Heaven when we die.

We can see that it follows the same thread - a belief that we will be taken away from earth; the place that God created for us to enjoy with Him.

The proposal is that at some point in the future all Christians will be transported to Heaven in order to save us from the forces of evil that are threatening to overpower us - the very forces that we are on earth to overcome.

From what we have discovered of the kingdom of God being established on earth and the fact that the enemy has already had his teeth pulled out, coupled with the fact that it is our responsibility to further expand God's kingdom on earth, we might realise that the doctrine must be incorrect, but many still cling to it and so we will carefully dismantle it here.

It is another ploy of the enemy that seeks to divert our attention from building God's kingdom on earth.

Why, if we are wandering around with our heads in the air, looking at the clouds above, waiting to be whisked away, would we be in the least bit interested in building the kingdom that Jesus taught His followers about?

The enemy continues to attempt to disrupt God's purposes.

The idea of a rapture was, quite rightly, strongly opposed by Charles Spurgeon, who lived during the same era as J. N. Darby.

However, this teaching has caught on amongst many Christian groups, and has spread far and wide, particularly among American evangelicals.

We have looked at some of these issues earlier but it won't hurt to go over them again, from a slightly different angle.

In order to discuss the rapture we need to think about Heaven - where and what it is.

Is it a place that exists in the sky somewhere?

Does Heaven have a geographical identity above our atmosphere or in the solar system?

Or does Heaven - the place where God lives, exist in another realm?

"Where is Heaven"? is a question that has been asked by many, for different reasons.

In the book of Acts we read that Stephen looked into Heaven.

But Stephen, full of the Holy Spirit, gazed steadily into Heaven and saw the glory of God, and he saw Jesus standing in the place of honour at God's right hand.
Acts of the Apostles 7:55.

Paul was also temporarily taken into Heaven:

I was caught up to the third Heaven fourteen years ago. Whether I was in my body or out of my body, I don't know—only God knows.

2 Corinthians 12:2.

John was also shown visions when he was taken into Heaven:

And instantly I was in the Spirit, and I saw a throne in Heaven and someone sitting on it.
Revelation 4:2.

As we have discussed previously, Heaven isn't far away from us at all.

The word rapture - *'rapere'* is latin in origin.

It is taken from the Greek word, *'harpagēsometha',* which is a word that appears only once in the original scriptures, in 1 Thessalonians, 4.17 of our Bibles, and means to be caught up, snatched or seized.

This is the only instance in scripture that we have anything, that is even vaguely, a reference to us being taken away.

The idea of a rapture has its roots in a misunderstanding of something that Paul was explaining to the Thessalonian Christians:

For the Lord himself will come down from Heaven with a commanding shout, with the voice of the archangel, and with the trumpet call of God. First, the believers who have died will rise from their graves.

Then, together with them, we who are still alive and remain on the earth will be caught up in the clouds to meet the Lord in the air.

Then we will be with the Lord forever.
1 Thessalonians 4:16-17.

Paul was writing about being caught up when the Lord returns in the clouds, which is another way of talking about Heaven - the clouds describe the place where God dwells.

Paul was explaining to the Christians that when the Lord returns, the dead in Christ will rise first, and will be transformed from death into life.

We will then all meet Jesus in the air.

It is the phrase, in the air that has caused some trouble.

So let's look at both of these phrases.

Firstly to be caught up, - *'rapere'.*

Paul is describing the act of being one with Jesus.

We will be gathered to Him - snatched away, - not to another place, but from whatever we are doing at that time.

Heaven will accompany Jesus, as it is the abode of God.

Jesus will appear from Heaven; which is where God lives - *'in our midst'*.

It will be a big event.

We will be enthralled by His presence and overtaken by it.

Jesus will be on centre stage.

Therefore we will all be seized by that scene.

All of which is incorporated in that word *'rapere'*.

Paul is not describing being taken from earth.

Indeed it might be strange that he would, as Jesus will have just returned to it, to claim His kingdom, as He promised His disciples that He would.

Paul is talking about being taken up by His presence.

Another word in discussion is the phrase, in the air.

As many Christians will have been buried for an unknown period of time it needs no explanation as to why Paul writes *'in the air'* on their behalf, but he is also alluding to the fact that we will be in the earth's atmosphere and not somewhere else.

In truth Paul is describing Jesus appearing on earth, having come from another realm - Heaven.

Jesus will be bringing Heaven to earth and not vice versa.

Paul was telling the Thessalonians that we will all be on earth, the dead and the living, in the earth's atmosphere (air), together with Jesus.

It is thought that the Thessalonian Christians were being taught incorrectly, that Jesus had already returned and that they had missed the event.

Paul was giving an answer to that misunderstanding.

Let us too spread the truth in order to dismantle those thoughts and doctrines that distract us from the purposes of God.

Paul felt so strongly about people spreading these false doctrines that he twice cursed anyone who preached them.

I am shocked that you are turning away so soon from God, who called you to himself through the loving mercy of Christ.

You are following a different way that pretends to be the Good News but is not the Good News at all.

You are being fooled by those who deliberately twist the truth concerning Christ.

Let God's curse fall on anyone, including us or even an angel from Heaven, who preaches a different kind of Good News than the one we preached to you.

I say again what we have said before: If anyone preaches any other Good News than the one you welcomed, let that person be cursed.
Galatians 1:6-9.

As we have seen earlier, Paul felt so strongly about these cancerous false doctrines, that he put Hymenaus, Philetus and Alexander out of fellowship until they had learned not to blaspheme.

It will be good for us too if we do not continue to spread a false gospel.

Tribulations.

God blesses those who patiently endure testing and temptation.

Afterward they will receive the crown of life that God has promised to those who love him.
James 1:12.

The warning of persecution, trials and tribulations are often mentioned in scripture.

Jesus warned that these trials would come but that we need not be concerned about them because He has overcome the world.

I have told you all this so that you may have peace in me. Here on earth you will have many trials and sorrows.

But take heart, because I have overcome the world."
John 16:33.

Indeed, were it not for the trials that we face daily, there would be no opportunity for us to be the victorious people who are the sons and daughters of God.

There may be fierce persecution of Christians at some period in the future which will be aggressive, but there is no threat involved in those tribulations that will overcome us.

But you belong to God, my dear children. You have already won a victory over those people, because the Spirit who lives in you is greater than the spirit who lives in the world.
1 John 4:4.

Jesus also talked to His followers about the times that would be before His return.

"Then you will be arrested, persecuted, and killed. You will be hated all over the world because you are my followers.

And many will turn away from me and betray and hate each other.
And many false prophets will appear and will deceive many people.

Sin will be rampant everywhere, and the love of many will grow cold.

But the one who endures to the end will be saved.

And the Good News about the Kingdom will be preached throughout the whole world, so that all nations will hear it; and then the end will come.
Matthew 24:9-14.

The end that Jesus was talking about is the end of opportunity to find Him for those who don't know Him already.

These are the times that many are afraid of - they are times that are spoken of with fear and awe.

It is because of these times that a doctrine of rapture was spoken of, as an escape from an imagined overwhelming period of tribulation.

But what does Jesus say about these times?

Jesus said that we will be able to endure these times and to be saved from them.

Jesus also said that whilst these trials are continuing the good news of the kingdom will be preached throughout the world.

This doesn't sound like a time that we need to be in awe of in a fearful way, but it sounds like a time to be rejoicing over - it is a time of victory and triumph.

We may be persecuted, but the enemy will be increasingly overcome and dispatched from the scene.

The earth will be restored, as will all of creation, as God's kingdom is established, and will be preached throughout the world.

Paul wrote to the Christians at Thessalonica and us, to be aware of the times, so that we wouldn't be taken by surprise by them, but for us not to be afraid of them.

But you aren't in the dark about these things, dear brothers and sisters, and you won't be surprised when the day of the Lord comes like a thief.

For you are all children of the light and of the day; we don't belong to darkness and night.
1 Thessalonians 5:4-5.

James spoke of times of tribulation with an eye to what these times produce in us:

Dear brothers and sisters, when troubles of any kind come your way, consider it an opportunity for great joy.

For you know that when your faith is tested, your endurance has a chance to grow.

So let it grow, for when your endurance is fully developed, you will be perfect and complete, needing nothing.
James 1:2-4.

Paul wrote to the Christians at Rome about the trials that lay ahead for them:

We can rejoice, too, when we run into problems and trials, for we know that they help us develop endurance.

And endurance develops strength of character, and character strengthens our confident hope of salvation.

And this hope will not lead to disappointment.

For we know how dearly God loves us, because he has given us the Holy Spirit to fill our hearts with his love. Romans 5:3-5.

We can be sure that, whilst trials and difficulties will be encountered in our life, we are also given the abilities to overcome them, and to endure through them.

It is only by encountering difficulties, whether they be confrontations with others, overcoming our own shortcomings or persecutions of a different kind, that we are able to face those difficulties, overcome them and to become mature to be fully grown sons and daughters of God.

A New Heaven and a New Earth.

There are some who preach that the universe that we live in - the creation of God, is to be destroyed and replaced with a completely new Heaven and a new earth.

They preach that God has given up on his first creation and is going to start again.

They have taken the symbolism that is to be found in the book of revelation and elsewhere in scripture, and applied it literally.

Let's look at some scriptures that tell us a different story.

We have previously discovered that Jesus will be revealed among His people on earth - that His kingdom will be established on earth.

In truth, we have discovered that Heaven will be joining us.

Let's look at where those, who preach of the earth's destruction, obtain their false information.

It is in the book of Revelation that a new Heaven and a new earth is mentioned.

The writer was describing, not a new creation, but a new and different situation existing between Heaven and earth.

We have found out that we are born again into God's kingdom in order to establish God's kingdom on earth.

We are continually invited into God's presence and we are able to come and go, to and from, Heaven as a consequence of the blood of Jesus that is our righteousness.

It was revealed to John, who was given the visions in the book of Revelation, what the situation will be when we take God at His word - when we take on God's righteousness in truth, and dwell with God.

Heaven will be merged with earth.

This will begin, not a new creation, but the restoration of the existing creation.

As I was reading chapter twenty one of the book of Revelation I found that there are no short verses that could be inserted here for explanation, but the chapter is filled with a glorious revelation - a description of the Bride of Christ living in unity with the God of creation.

This chapter is all about God, living with His people.

I will open this chapter up with some insights when you have read through.

1. Then I saw a new Heaven and a new earth, for the old Heaven and the old earth had disappeared. And the sea was also gone.

2. And I saw the holy city, the new Jerusalem, coming down from God out of Heaven like a bride beautifully dressed for her husband.

I heard a loud shout from the throne, saying, "Look, God's home is now among his people!

He will live with them, and they will be his people. God himself will be with them. He will wipe every tear from their eyes, and there will be no more death or sorrow or crying or pain.

All these things are gone forever." And the one sitting on the throne said, "Look, I am making everything new!" And then he said to me, "Write this down, for what I tell you is trustworthy and true."

And he also said, "It is finished! I am the Alpha and the Omega—the Beginning and the End.

To all who are thirsty I will give freely from the springs of the water of life.

7. All who are victorious will inherit all these blessings, and I will be their God, and they will be my children.

"But cowards, unbelievers, the corrupt, murderers, the immoral, those who practice witchcraft, idol worshipers, and all liars—their fate is in the fiery lake of burning sulphur. This is the second death."

9. Then one of the seven angels who held the seven bowls containing the seven last plagues came and said to me, "Come with me! I will show you the bride, the wife of the Lamb."

So he took me in the Spirit to a great, high mountain, and he showed me the holy city, Jerusalem, descending out of Heaven from God. It shone with the glory of God and sparkled like a precious stone—like jasper as clear as crystal.

The city wall was broad and high, with twelve gates guarded by twelve angels.

And the names of the twelve tribes of Israel were written on the gates.

13. There were three gates on each side—east, north, south, and west. The wall of the city had twelve foundation stones, and on them were written the names of the twelve apostles of the Lamb.

The angel who talked to me held in his hand a gold measuring stick to measure the city, its gates, and its wall.

When he measured it, he found it was a square, as wide as it was long. In fact, its length and width and height were each 1,400 miles. Then he measured the walls and found them to be 216 feet thick (according to the human standard used by the angel).

The wall was made of jasper, and the city was pure gold, as clear as glass. The wall of the city was built on foundation stones inlaid with twelve precious stones: the first was jasper, the second sapphire, the third agate, the fourth emerald, the fifth onyx, the sixth carnelian, the seventh chrysolite, the eighth beryl, the ninth topaz, the tenth chrysoprase, the eleventh jacinth, the twelfth amethyst.

The twelve gates were made of pearls—each gate from a single pearl! And the main street was pure gold, as clear as glass.

I saw no temple in the city, for the Lord God Almighty and the Lamb are its temple.

And the city has no need of sun or moon, for the glory of God illuminates the city, and the Lamb is its light.

The nations will walk in its light, and the kings of the world will enter the city in all their glory.

Its gates will never be closed at the end of day because there is no night there. And all the nations will bring their glory and honour into the city.

27. *Nothing evil will be allowed to enter, nor anyone who practices shameful idolatry and dishonesty—but only those whose names are written in the Lamb's Book of Life.*
Revelation 21:1̶27.

Isn't that a wonderful picture?

My attention was drawn to verse one, which exclaims that all the sea was gone.

The sea, in scripture, symbolises a state of uneasiness - a tension or restlessness and strife, among the nations.

We are not being told that the literal seas will disappear, but that the tensions on earth are no more - Jesus is reigning, in peace.

In verse two, the New Jerusalem - the city of God, is how the Bride of Christ is described - we are the new Jerusalem and it is us who are arising - out of God, from Heaven, the place that has become our home.

We have discussed the rewards given to those who are victorious, previously.

Here, in verse seven, we find them being honoured.

In verse nine, John was invited to see the Bride:

"Come with me! I will show you the bride, the wife of the Lamb.

But it is not a female that John is shown, but a city - the city that is coming down from Heaven is not a literal city made from stone and earthly materials, but it is a spiritual city.

The city is the *'ekklesia'* of God.

John is then shown the measurements and other notable facts about how the city - the Bride, is put together.

It is interesting to note, in verse thirteen, that there are doors or gates, in the walls of the city.

We might wonder, what is the purpose of these gates?

Does it have anything to do with verse twenty seven -

27. Nothing evil will be allowed to enter, nor anyone who practices shameful idolatry and dishonesty—but only those whose names are written in the Lamb's Book of Life.

In the vision that John relates there are clearly those who are not a part of the city, who live outside.

If this was a description of a completely new creation, after the earth had been destroyed, as some suggest, would there still be those living outside who are not a part of the Bride?

I think not.

Rather, the vision that John is given, is of the Bride and the Groom - Jesus is the Groom - Heaven and His Bride, on earth, becoming one.

It is a time that is not too distant from today - it is a time when the body of Christ has put away the unrighteousness that presently pervades the lives of the sons and daughters of God.

It is a time when we have robed ourselves in righteousness, in order to be worthy of the Groom, who is Jesus.

It is a time when the Groom and the Bride have become one.

That time could be now, had we paid attention to the call of Jesus - had we responded to the letters written to the various groups, in the first four chapters of the book of Revelation.

There are those who are living outside of the City of God who are not a part of that union.

And yet, there are doors or gates within the walls of the city that would allow access, should there be those who wish to enter.

In truth, the vision describes the period that we are living in.

Jesus is described as the gate, in the good news of John, chapter ten:

Yes, I am the gate. Those who come in through me will be saved.
They will come and go freely and will find good pastures.
John 10:9.

Therefore, John's vision must be a picture of the period we are entering into now - a time when we become one with the Godhead in reality - a time when Heaven becomes one with earth.

When Jesus is revealed in God's Kingdom on earth there will be some who are not one with that unity - outside the gates of the city, as there are today.

There are some today, who are preaching about the imminent end of the earth.

They point to the many ecological and man made disasters that are occurring during this time, in order to justify their prophecies of doom.

What of the destruction or demise of earth?

What does scripture tell us about this?

We can perhaps appreciate, from our reading of previous chapters, that this might not be the case.

There are numerous scriptures that give the instruction for the recipients, and also to us, to *'be fruitful and to multiply'*.

Christians are born into the kingdom of God in order to reproduce others, who also represent Jesus.

We will also reproduce Jesus in our work and social lives when we spend time with Him - this is how the kingdom is established on earth.

In the book of Genesis we read many times with regards to life giving birth to life, seed producing seed etc.

The earth has within it a God given mandate to be fruitful and to reproduce.

Then God blessed them and said, "Be fruitful and multiply.
Fill the earth and govern it.

Reign over the fish in the sea, the birds in the sky, and all the animals that scurry along the ground."
Genesis 1:28.

Nowhere, at any time, has this commission been taken away or altered.

There is perpetuity built into that process.

We have been given the responsibility for allowing reproductive activity to happen on earth.

For the earth will be filled with the knowledge of the glory of the Lord as the waters cover the sea.
Habakkuk 2:14 NIV

In spite of what some preachers, the newspapers and media tell us, with regards to the final days of earth, The Bible is filled with references to earth being restored and renewed.

Paul explained to the Christians in Rome that earth was waiting for a restoration.

For all creation is waiting eagerly for that future day when God will reveal who his children really are.

Against its will, all creation was subjected to God's curse.

But with eager hope, the creation looks forward to the day when it will join God's children in glorious freedom from death and decay.
Romans 8:21.

The prophet Isaiah often prophesied about the earth being renewed:

Even the wilderness and desert will be glad in those days.

The wasteland will rejoice and blossom with spring crocuses.
Yes, there will be an abundance of flowers and singing and joy!

The deserts will become as green as the mountains of Lebanon, as lovely as Mount Carmel or the plain of Sharon. There the Lord will display his glory, the splendour of our God.

With this news, strengthen those who have tired hands, and encourage those who have weak knees.

Say to those with fearful hearts, "Be strong, and do not fear, for your God is coming to destroy your enemies. He is coming to save you."

And when he comes, he will open the eyes of the blind and unplug the ears of the deaf.

The lame will leap like a deer, and those who cannot speak will sing for joy!

Springs will gush forth in the wilderness, and streams will water the wasteland.

The parched ground will become a pool, and springs of water will satisfy the thirsty land.

Marsh grass and reeds and rushes will flourish where desert jackals once lived. And a great road will go through that once deserted land. It will be named the Highway of Holiness.

Evil-minded people will never travel on it.

It will be only for those who walk in God's ways; fools will never walk there.

Lions will not lurk along its course, nor any other ferocious beasts.
There will be no other dangers.

Only the redeemed will walk on it.
Those who have been ransomed by the Lord will return.

They will enter Jerusalem singing, crowned with everlasting joy. Sorrow and mourning will disappear, and they will be filled with joy and gladness.
Isaiah 35:1-10.

"But forget all that— it is nothing compared to what I am going to do. For I am about to do something new.

And on another occasion:

See, I have already begun!

Do you not see it?
I will make a pathway through the wilderness.
I will create rivers in the dry wasteland.

The wild animals in the fields will thank me, the jackals and owls, too, for giving them water in the desert.

Yes, I will make rivers in the dry wasteland so my chosen people can be refreshed.
Isaiah 43:18-20.

Isaiah was talking about very present difficulties that are causing concern on the earth today and assuring us of the restoration that will come.

When you give them your breath, life is created, and you renew the face of the earth.

May the glory of the Lord continue forever! The Lord takes pleasure in all he has made!
Psalms 104:30-31.

The Lord takes pleasure in all that He has made.

In truth the Lord cannot change His mind - He has no need to, he is aware of circumstance and has already planned ahead for every situation.

Then God looked over all he had made, and he saw that it was very good!
Genesis 1:31.

From the beginning God saw that all that He had made was good, He has no need to alter that opinion.

For as the waters fill the sea, the earth will be filled with an awareness of the glory of the Lord.
Habakkuk 2:14.

The days of creation.

"You are worthy, O Lord our God, to receive glory and honour and power. For you created all things, and they exist because you created what you pleased."
Revelation 4:11.

I would be surprised if any single subject has caused so much division in the body of Christ, and also ridicule from those who are in the world, as the description of the creation that is found in the book of Genesis.

As Christians we might expect ridicule, but does our explanation of the act of creation by God unnecessarily fuel the fire of scorn?

Ridicule from the world can be expected as a response to a life lived in faith, but with regards to the claims of creation that some have been heard to make, is there justification?

There is quite a widely held belief that the universe has evolved over several millennia.

The first chapter of the book of Genesis - a book of beginnings, gives a very precise and clear description of how the earth and all of creation were created by God in six days.

Therefore, there is some disparity between those who take the Bible that has been translated for us as the word of God which can not be disputed, and others, who do not.

The description of the creation, in the first chapter of Genesis, reads like a poem or a marching song.

It is as if someone had written it down in verse form in order for others to recite and memorise the main facts.

It is believed that it was Moses who wrote down the events that we find in Genesis, whilst wandering in the desert after leaving Egypt with the Israelites.

When we look into the recital more closely we can find three phrases that periodically repeat, as if in the refrain of a chorus between verses.

These repetitions are:

1. *And that is what happened……*

2. *And evening passed and morning came, marking the …… day.*

3. *And God saw that it was good.*

It is thought that Moses may have written these verses down in the way that he has in order to teach the Israelites, who had been recently released from slavery, about the foundations of their past.

I can well imagine the Israelites singing the song as they marched through the desert, with raised voices, as the repeated phrases were sung.

If I were Moses, writing a book about the foundations of the universe, I might also include a song that I had written, to remind others of the main facts.

There is a significant amount of understanding that we might glean, when we read about the placing of numbers within scripture.

Numbers tell us a story of their own.

The number two, for example, speaks about agreement and witness.

The number six is the number of man's achievements, outside of God.

The number three speaks to us about strength and unity.

The number seven, which is the number of days that Moses has accounted for the creation of the universe, speaks to us about perfection and the works of God.

In accounting for the period of creation, Moses is telling us, amongst other things, that all that God created is perfect in every way.

We have been assured that the timing of God, in creation, is perfect.

The word, day, that we read in these verses is loosely translated from the Hebrew word *'Yom'*.

Exactly the same form of the word has also been translated elsewhere in Genesis as aeon, an era, an unspecified period of time and an age.

It can also be translated as, *during the days of, ages, days,* and *day of the days.*

The word, *'Yom'* is listed as no. 3117 in Strong's dictionary of Bible words.

It is a word of Hebrew origin that has been used no less than 2,303 times in scripture and in various ways, depending upon how the person translating the scripture believed it should be placed.

In order to give us some understanding of the way that the different variations of the word have been used, I have placed a short list here.

Variations and even direct translations, from this word or phrase, can be made as follows, depending upon the understood context:

afternoon, all, always, amount, battle, birthday,
completely, continually, course, daily, daily the days,

day, day of the days, day that the period, day's, daylight, days, days on the day, days to day, days you shall daily, days ago, days', each , each day, entire, eternity, evening, ever in your life, every day, fate, first, forever, forevermore, full, full year, future, holiday, later, length, life, lifetime, lifetime, live, long, long as i live, long, midday, now, older, once, period, perpetually, present, recently, reigns, ripe, short-lived, so long, some time, survived, time, time, times, today, today, usual, very old, when, when the days, whenever, while, whole, year, yearly, years, yesterday.

We can see that when reading any version of scripture we must be very aware that we place ourselves very much in the hand of whoever has translated that particular piece of script.

We must be very careful not to be dogmatic about our own particular revelation, or understanding of the Bible that is in front of us.

Our arrogance - stubbornness, with regards to correction or to allow any other realisation to enter our consciousness can, and has, caused much harm to the unity of the body.

Often, the stance we take has little to do with faith and much to do with obstinacy.

The determination of some to demand that God created the Heavens and the earth within a stipulated period of

146

time has been a source of much merriment and ridicule in the world.

It has also been the source of division and alienation in the body, which not only prevents the growth and maturity of the majority, but also serves the enemy very well.

We are called to harmony:

Do all that you can to live in peace with everyone.
Romans 12:18.

As if to confirm that the first chapter is simply a recital of a memorable poem, in chapter two Moses introduces us to an alternative version of the events of the creation, with the animals having been created after man:

Then the Lord God said, "It is not good for the man to be alone. I will make a helper who is just right for him."
Genesis 2:18.

In chapter one we have the man and woman created last as the crowning glory of all of creation and in chapter two we read that the animals are created later.

There are wider explanations for this second, alternative version, but one might wonder why Moses chose to write it down twice.

I have no quarrel at all, with those who dogmatically defend the theory that the creation was fulfilled in six precise days.

I am sure that wouldn't be a problem for God.

However, the suggestion does seem out of character to me.

My own understanding, given that the translation of the Hebrew word for day - *'yom',* can be translated in terms of a longer or unknown period of time, is that of a loving creator, who is known to be both patient and thorough.

We know that it was He who spoke creation into being.

He is not one to wave a magic wand for everything to suddenly appear, in my experience.

We can read, in John's good news, that the word, who is Jesus, was in the beginning.

In the beginning the Word already existed.
The Word was with God, and the Word was God.
He existed in the beginning with God.

God created everything through him, and nothing was created except through him.

The Word gave life to everything that was created, and his life brought light to everyone.

The light shines in the darkness, and the darkness can never extinguish it.
John 1:1-5.

All of creation was given life through Jesus.

My experience of God's dealings with mankind is one of slow deliberate activity.

He is not impatient.

With regards to the return of Jesus, Peter writes:

The Lord isn't really being slow about his promise, as some people think. No, he is being patient for your sake. He does not want anyone to be destroyed, but wants everyone to repent.
2 Peter 3:9.

I was not a witness during the works of the creation and so have limited access to knowledge of the processes involved, but my impression is that God set His creation in motion.

He is the initiator - another way to translate the phrase that we have as, *'in the beginning, God created'*, in the book of Genesis, is, *'God began a process of creation'*.

We can understand then, that the phrase introduces for us a picture of the creation being a continual process.

God is the producer, or an initiator of a process, that culminated in the production of man.

I am confident that during the process of creation there were times when adjustments and changes were made along the way - as a gardener might prune and weed a flower bed.

Or, as a potter produces a clay pot.

And yet, O Lord, you are our Father.

We are the clay, and you are the potter.
We all are formed by your hand.
Isaiah 64:8.

There is time allowed in creation for the laying down of fossil fuels, iron ore and pockets of valuable gems to be stored away, for our use when we might use them at a later date.

We can read in the book of Genesis that God breathed life into man.

Then the Lord God formed the man from the dust of the ground.

He breathed the breath of life into the man's nostrils, and the man became a living person.
Genesis 2:7.

I believe that this is the shortest account of the evolution of man that we know.

It is probably all we need to know with regards to the origin of man.

But we might like to look at some explanations and to expand the dialogue.

After Jesus was resurrected from the dead, we read in John's gospel, a similar event that occurred:

Then he breathed on them and said, "Receive the Holy Spirit.
John 20:22.

It was similar in that on both occasions a new creation - new life was created.

On the first occasion life was breathed into Adam.

On the second occasion, the disciples, and by extension, we, were given life - we became a new, living breathing body.

This means that anyone who belongs to Christ has become a new person. The old life is gone; a new life has begun!
2 Corinthians 5:17.

We are a new creation - the old man is dead and the new man is alive.

The point about this is that we once had an old body - it was a dead body, living in corruption and death, but it existed.

We don't refer to our old life, we talk about our new life in Christ, but the old life did exist.

When the Lord breathed life into us we became a new creation - a new man, - the old has now gone, as if it never existed, to be remembered no more.

Adam too became the first man - he was a new creation. Nothing like Adam had ever existed before the Lord breathed life into him.

I may get shot for suggesting this but, I wonder if Adam too had a history, stretching back, perhaps for millions of years.

I wonder if Adam, like us, arrived at a point in time when he could appreciate and recognise that there was a creator, and that he wanted to know Him.

Was it at this time that our Creator took the old Adam, who had grown from the dust of the earth, as the book of Genesis describes, and breathed new life into him in order to produce a new man, in His own image?

We don't talk about the old man but we look only at the new creation - it is the new creation that is the focus for us.

Adam was God's new creation.

We don't know the circumstances, our translators, perhaps under some pressure from either those in authority over them, or as a result of peer pressure, have placed their own slant on the text in our Bibles.

It is worth mentioning that neither palaeontologists, archaeologists or scientists have arrived at any positive conclusions with regards to the evolution of mankind.

There are gaps that cannot be resolved, in the theoretical sequence of events, of an evolution through to present day humanity.

There is agreement amongst these, very well educated and experienced people, that something unexplainable must have occurred in order for man to have leapt from one state of being, to the modern man that we now are.

They scratch their heads, unable to explain the speed of the increase in development - they agree that, from what they know, the development was not naturally possible.

There are missing ingredients in the evolution of man that can only be explained by the presence of God.

Biologists explain, and I have no reason to disbelieve them, that two different sexual species occurred some two and a half billion years ago.

These species are called *eukaryotic* and were the first creatures that required two opposite sexes in order to mate and reproduce.

I was not there and have a limited understanding of biology.

But for me this indicates a time where God had nudged creation in order to produce two different sexes.

God arranged for it to be necessary for there to be two sexes in order for us to mate and reproduce. That is the way that He has approved and designed it.

There is a lot that we can discuss with regards to there only being two different sexes, but we won't dwell on it here, we will move on.

The description that we have in the book of Genesis, far from disagreeing with the science, confirms and adds more explanation than the biologists, palaeontologists, scientists and archaeologists have to hand.

Our account in the book of Genesis explains that it was necessary to take something from the male in order to create the female.

Moses has described this something as a rib, which is fine.

Whether the original writings, or God's advice to Moses, referred to a rib or another part of man can be debated at length, the exact detail is quite possibly not relevant for us to know.

It is possible that Moses was able to refer to older manuscripts that we know nothing about.

The account that we have in Genesis describes the creator dividing the woman from the man.

We are told that all of creation was for our purpose:

Then God blessed them and said, "Be fruitful and multiply. Fill the earth and govern it.

Reign over the fish in the sea, the birds in the sky, and all the animals that scurry along the ground."

Then God said, "Look! I have given you every seed-bearing plant throughout the earth and all the fruit trees for your food.

And I have given every green plant as food for all the wild animals, the birds in the sky, and the small animals that scurry along the ground—everything that has life." And that is what happened.
Genesis 1:30.

There are many today who claim that mankind are usurpers on the earth and that the earth would be better off if we were not here, but that is not what God said and it is not His intention to remove us from it:

In truth, creation was put in place for us to enjoy, within the guidelines that He put in place.

We are responsible for the earth - for its well being, and we will learn to govern and to reign over it correctly when our thoughts, words and actions are aligned with the creator.

We live in an age that is very distant from these events and we have no personal witnesses to confirm any of our assumptions, apart from God's Spirit within us.

There is very much more to be gained in realising that our unity is of far more value than our fragmentation.

A day is coming when we will know all things.

To be dogmatic with regards to our beliefs without having definitive clarity given to us by God's Spirit, is simply foolish and leads us to a dead end spiritually, and often, physically.

The enemy loves to redirect our focus, by filling our lives with dead ends and red herrings.

We have discovered that Jesus will not return to His kingdom until He is revealed to the world among the sons and daughters who know Him.

This needs to be our aim and we should not waste our time with pointless quests.

We might wonder how a disunified body will be able to preach unity and oneness to a broken world when we are in such disarray ourselves.

There is much to do with regards to repairing the disunity that is currently accepted as the norm amongst us.

God's kingdom will not be preached to the world from a platform of unrighteousness and disunity.

This will continue until we all come to such unity in our faith and knowledge of God's Son that we will be mature in the Lord, measuring up to the full and complete standard of Christ.
Ephesians 4:13.

Church.

We might be coming to the conclusion that the translation of scriptures can be a very personalised task.

The translators will take up a section of scripture and use their understanding to interpret the meaning into words that they can relate to in their own language.

As we have seen with the thief on the cross event, this understanding can cause the translation to be limited to a personal belief, and in some instances cause much misunderstanding, unless we are nudged into a better revelation by God's Spirit.

Another situation where this problem has occured is where our translators have given us the word, church in our Bibles.

It was Jesus who first introduced the concept of a group of people who had been called out of the world for a specific purpose and who belonged to Him.

Jesus told Peter that the *'ekklesia'* of God', would be built upon a foundation of the revelation of who Jesus is.

'Upon this rock (of revelation), I will build my church (ekklesia').
Matthew 16:18. (para).

For some of us, the word church conjures up images of brick or stone buildings.

For others it might release images of many people throughout the ages who belong to the Lord.

A few of us might even be aware that the word church should not be found in our Bibles at all.

The word is another mistranslation.

But more importantly for us, as we look closer into this phenomenon that is church, we might find that the systems and organisations that comprise our modern churches and denominations are also operated on unscriptural lines, in that they follow doctrines and traditions that are nowhere to be found in scripture.

This cannot be true! I hear you shout.

I can identify with your cynicism and, knowing many who attend church each week and who are a part of that system, I can readily agree that it is difficult to accept that the claim could be true and the idea of church being outside of God's kingdom must be simply preposterous.

Isn't it?

We can but begin at the beginning and work our way through, to find out if this is a correct claim.

Most of us will want to skip the first few pages, with regards to how the name, church, came into being, this is old hat, for us, but read further.

Our word, church, comes originally from the Greek word, *'kyriakos'* and means, belonging to a lord, and later, from the Anglo Saxon word, *'circe'*, *'circol'*, which is where our words circle and circus also come from.

The word church had been in our vocabulary long before King James insisted on its insertion in our Bibles and was previously used to describe a place of pagan worship.

These were almost invariably situated in a circular formation as can be witnessed in the Stonehenge stone circle, hence the reference to the Anglo Saxon words, *'circe'* and *'circol'*.

We can discover a lot about a thing by uncovering its roots.

'Kyriakos' is a word that only occurs twice in the original Greek text that our Bibles have been translated from, and nowhere does it refer to the children of God.

These are:

When you meet together, you are not really interested in the Lord's Supper.
1 Corinthians 11:20.

(The meal that belongs to the Lord).

And:

It was the lord's Day, and I was worshipping in the Spirit. Suddenly, I heard behind me a loud voice like a trumpet blast.
Revelation 1:10.

The latter reference to the lord's day is thought to be a reference, not to a specific day belonging to our Lord, but to a day that was set aside by the Romans to worship their god's, hence, the lord's or, the god's day.

We will take a look at why our translators have chosen to use the word *'kyriakos'* rather than the word that Jesus used, *'ekklesia',* in due course.

For those who would like a deeper look into this concept of church I would direct you to a fascinating study that has been carried out, giving far more insight than is relevant here:
https://calendarofscripture.com/2016/12/24/etymology-of-the-word-church/

The Greek word, *'Kyriakos'* was also taken by Scottish communities and incorporated into their language.

It is where we get the word, Kirk (*Kirke*). *A word that means,* all that is owned by a local lord or laird.

This would include all of the woodland, open land, and the men, women and children who worked on the estate.

The word '*Kyriakos*', means belonging to a lord.

But '*kyriakos*' *is* not the word that Jesus used.

It was King James who directed the translators not to use the term that Jesus used, which was '*ekklesia*', but to use the term church instead.

They could have used the English words, gathering, or assembly, but they didn't.

The first time that the idea of a gathering of people, who would later be called Christians in the scriptures, came whilst Jesus was talking to His disciples about receiving revelation.

Jesus said to Peter:

*Now I say to you that you are Peter (which means 'rock'), and upon this rock I will build my church, **(ekklesia)**, and all the powers of hell will not conquer it. Matthew 16:18.*

Jesus referred to Peter as a rock - The Greek word, *'Petra',* means rock.

This was a play on words, Jesus was fond of playing with language.

But Jesus was referring to the rock of revelation that the *'ekklesia'* would be built upon - the revelation of who Jesus is.

Peter had just received such a revelation.

Simon Peter answered, "You are the Messiah, the Son of the living God."
Matthew 16:16.

The Greek word, *'ekklesia',* is written one hundred and fifteen times in the original scriptures.

One hundred and thirteen of those occasions is with a reference to the body of believers.

But our translators have chosen not to use this original word, but to replace it with the Greek word, *'kyriakos'.*

We can go through our Bibles and erase the word church from them completely.

We could replace it with a phrase such as, the believers, or people who have a purpose or the people of the way, as they were known at that time.

But why did the translators change the word?

What does the word, *'ekklesia',* that Jesus used, really mean?

We can understand why and how our translators of the King James Bible believed that church would be a good substitution for the word *'ekklesia'.*

When we place ourselves in their situation and look around, we can understand that all they were aware of was the powerful religious organisations of the day - the rigid, powerful, ecclesiastical structures of administration, the stone, temple-like buildings that housed them and the congregations who were spectators within them.

There was nothing else for them to assess what Jesus was referring to but what they knew existed at that time.

What had the name of Christianity in those dark days was called church, and therefore the translators of the day transferred what they knew then, to the words of Jesus - that was what existed then and therefore they came to the conclusion that must be the correct translation.

In truth, had the translators of that time given a different understanding of the word *'ekklesia',* there might have been some severe consequences for them.

'*Kyriakos*' was their best, and in truth, the only way they understood the concept could be translated.

To talk about a group of people who were free from the restraints of religious administration - free from religious worship - free from the restraints of gathering within church buildings and free to worship without leadership oversight, would not have gone down well with those in authority in the age that the translators of the King James Bible were working.

But that is not what the words of Jesus were, and what church was then, and what it has become now, has very little to do with the kingdom life that Jesus was referring to.

But why have our present day translators continued to translate the words of Jesus in the same way?

To be fair to our modern day translators, the word, '*ekklesia*' is a difficult concept to explain in a single word - our English language does not have a single word to explain the idea of '*ekklesia*'.

It is a word that was originally coined to describe a group of people who might be called out for a specific duty, such as jury service or to take part in a public meeting or with reference to a group of people who had been selected to take up arms against an enemy.

It can be used to describe a gathering or an assembly of people.

The term, 'a called out people' has also been used to describe the *'ekklesia'* of God.

When we look a little closer at the denominational assemblies of today we might come to the conclusion that the *'ekklesia'* are those who have been called out from church organisations.

The *'ekklesia'* of God are a people who have been called out for a specific service.

We are called out in order to establish God's kingdom on earth.

As we read on we might begin to find that our understanding of church does not fit squarely with the *'ekklesia'* that Jesus was referring to.

In order to justify that statement we must draw up some comparisons.

We can do that by looking into the past.

The writer to the Hebrews gives us some clues as to the difference between the church that we know today and the *'ekklesia'* that Jesus spoke of:

The letter that was written to the Hebrews carried with it considerable comparisons that were made between the Old Covenant of Moses and the Tabernacle and the New Covenant that is made freely available to us through the blood of Jesus.

That first covenant between God and Israel had regulations for worship and a place of worship here on earth.
There were two rooms in that Tabernacle.
In the first room were a lampstand, a table, and sacred loaves of bread on the table. This room was called the Holy Place.
Then there was a curtain, and behind the curtain was the second room called the Most Holy Place.

In that room were a gold incense altar and a wooden chest called the Ark of the Covenant, which was covered with gold on all sides. Inside the Ark were a gold jar containing manna, Aaron's staff that sprouted leaves, and the stone tablets of the covenant.

Above the Ark were the cherubim of divine glory, whose wings stretched out over the Ark's cover, the place of atonement.
But we cannot explain these things in detail now.
When these things were all in place, the priests regularly entered the first room as they performed their religious duties.

But only the high priest ever entered the Most Holy Place, and only once a year.

And he always offered blood for his own sins and for the sins the people had committed in ignorance.

By these regulations the Holy Spirit revealed that the entrance to the Most Holy Place was not freely open as long as the Tabernacle and the system it represented were still in use.
This is an illustration pointing to the present time.

For the gifts and sacrifices that the priests offer are not able to cleanse the consciences of the people who bring them.
For that old system deals only with food and drink and various cleansing ceremonies—physical regulations that were in effect only until a better system could be established.
Hebrews 9:1-10.

We are reading about the Tabernacle that was built under the Old Covenant.

This was where worship took place before Solomon built the temple.

It described a situation where there were two rooms - the Holy Place and the Most Holy Place.

Only the Priests, who were Levites, could enter the Holy Place and only the High Priest could enter the Most Holy Place and only once each year, on the Day of Atonement.

Today, many churches follow a similar theme, whether they be modern, charismatic groups or age old traditional denominations.

A special place is reserved for leaders and the choir, who are set apart from the rest of the congregation.

Worship is conducted by the leaders, whilst the congregation look on, joining in with the singing.

It is the leaders who prompt the congregation, or spectators, into the presence of God.

Many churches also wear particular clothes, whether it be robes, gowns and uniforms or suits, white shirts and ties.

There is also a place for particularly special objects - incense burners, holy water, banners, flags, crosses, altars, tablecloths, stained glass windows, arcs, icons and many other things which often are meant to hold special powers or are deemed necessary for the purpose of 'worship'.

The writer of the Hebrews letter described the many components of the Tabernacle but did not explain their meaning.

Each one was a picture describing some aspect of the life and work of Jesus or warning the nation to remember the consequences of rebellion.

But they all pointed forward to the New Covenant which Jesus introduced.

That is why they are no longer needed today.

The New Covenant is here. We do not need to look forward to it any longer.

At that time the presence of God stayed in the Most Holy Place where the High Priest could enter once a year to sacrifice for his sin and the sins of the nation.

It was a solemn occasion, tinged with fear that the High Priest would not be alive when he came out.

So much so that a cord was tied to his ankle so that he could be pulled out of the tent if he died, without the need for any other person to enter the Most Holy Place.

Despite its pomp and ceremony, the Old Covenant was ineffective in reconciling man with God.

The singing was powerful.

When the Temple was finally built, there were choirs and musicians playing twenty four hours each day.

Many today also live their lives with Christian music being continually piped to their ears.

But all of this worship was only a shadow of what God was preparing for us.

Today, when we concentrate so much on singing songs and great musical bands, we remain under the Old Covenant, even though we enjoy the experience.

It is an act that feeds our emotions but has little to do with worship, and by following another person's lead or inspiration, we starve our own Spirit of the growth that only the Spirit of God can give through personal interaction and by responding to Him.

Instead we respond to a leader or leaders or a dedicated praise group as the temple worshippers of old would have done.

Jesus said:

But the time is coming—indeed it's here now—when true worshipers will worship the Father in spirit and in truth.

The Father is looking for those who will worship him that way.

John 4:23.

Let us read some more of the letter to the Hebrews:

So Christ has now become the High Priest over all the good things that have come.

He has entered that greater, more perfect Tabernacle in Heaven, which was not made by human hands and is not part of this created world.

With his own blood—not the blood of goats and calves—he entered the Most Holy Place once for all time and secured our redemption forever.

Under the old system, the blood of goats and bulls and the ashes of a heifer could cleanse people's bodies from ceremonial impurity.

Just think how much more the blood of Christ will purify our consciences from sinful deeds so that we can worship the living God.

For by the power of the eternal Spirit, Christ offered himself to God as a perfect sacrifice for our sins.
That is why he is the one who mediates a new covenant between God and people, so that all who are called can receive the eternal inheritance God has promised them.

For Christ died to set them free from the penalty of the sins they had committed under that first covenant.
Hebrews 9:11-15.

The old Tabernacle was made by human hands and was just an image of the spiritual one made by God.

The new Tabernacle is spiritual and does not need the earthly imitation of rituals, leaders and places to worship that were detailed in the Old Covenant.

God no longer requires religious services as an act of worship.

He has replaced that system with His New Covenant.

The Old Covenant required the people to pay a tithe in order to support the religious priestly order.

Many churches today also demand a tithe, a subscription or an offering in order to support the organisation or system that they belong to.

It is good to be generous with our time and finances - to give to those who need what we have in abundance - we are here to assist those in need, but there is no requirement for us to support an organisation that is outside of God's kingdom and intent on keeping its members within a form of religion that man alone has constructed around himself.

If we have come into the kingdom of God, we are owned 100% by Father.

Our finances along with everything else become wholly submitted to Him, there is no requirement for us to pay a fee to be a part of who He is.

Our redemption was 100% freely given.

When the tabernacle was built it became the focus of the nation of Israel and beyond, to the nations that surrounded them.

Although it was only a shadow of the New Covenant it had the singular purpose of attracting the attention of the world.

The man centred church systems that exist today exclaim to the world that we are a divided and disunified body.

There is much pride in the manner in which we adhere to and describe our church.

The many church organisations today are similar to a large family who are unable to live in the same house.

The Lord is not pleased with us because we all live in different rooms and don't speak to each other.

There are some who claim that the different gatherings are a result of the desire to bring a different form of worship - that each group has its own way of expressing itself.

This is very true, when we choose to go our own way it is called rebellion - we want to do things our way.

The difficulty with this claim is that it is not our expression of worship that the Lord requires, but it is His expression of worship that we ought to bring.

In truth we are not bringing different forms of expression of the body but different forms of our rebellious nature - we are declaring that we are right and they are not.

Being one with each other is not about our own comfort in the way we worship, but about living together in love.

Those who are more mature in the faith, - elders, have a responsibility to train each one of us towards growth.

Their responsibility is to equip God's people to do his work and build up the church, the body of Christ.

This will continue until we all come to such unity in our faith and knowledge of God's Son that we will be mature in the Lord, measuring up to the full and complete standard of Christ.
Ephesians 4:13.

Instead of this, the church congregation, or spectators, as I refer to them, are fed on milk, starved of spiritual food, they are not allowed to minister to each other and are kept in order by the unspoken rule that they are not to socialise or meet with Christians outside of the church circle.

This system of administration is so very far from the *'ekklesia'* that Jesus spoke to Peter and His followers about.

In today's church systems there is much peer pressure to stay inside the group or membership.

There is little opportunity to meet with others - to understand or to become involved in what the Lord might be doing elsewhere.

There is little opportunity to share life with others outside of the hours of service or meeting places.

We are all too familiar with the acts of hypocrisy, corruption, pornography, adultery, theft, disagreements and unrighteousness amongst leadership and also within the church congregations.

These should not be the acts of the called out people of God.

We should not be surprised by these things though, because church systems, whether they are modern, so called, 'spirit filled' groups, or creaking and aged denominations, in contrast to the way the *'ekklesia'* are taught to be, are administered on very similar lines as the world's other forms of businesses, industry and government.

There is a system of hierarchy - a structure of employment, qualifications are required to enter the system, there are wage structures, promotion is assessed by way of performance, there is encouragement to become the top person in the hierarchy.

There is no place in that hierarchy for those who are not qualified by man.

Are we beginning to understand why, in the book of Revelation, John records a voice saying:

Then I heard another voice calling from Heaven, "Come away from her, my people. Do not take part in her sins, or you will be punished with her.
Revelation 18:4.

The voice is speaking about Babylon, which is a term used when referring to all the world's systems that are set up in opposition to God's Kingdom and includes the world's organisations - man centred systems, whether they be religious, industrial, governmental, large or small and everything that is contrary and exists in rebellion to the kingdom of God.

There can be few situations where so many of God's people are caught up within a system other than the church of today, without being aware of the danger we are in by staying within it.

We can conclude that the voice from Heaven is including the present day church denominations in that call to come out of her.

Where else do we find God's people gathered in large numbers?

Today is a good time to come out of those systems while we have the opportunity to do so.

We can understand that the Lord is not calling us to be cut off from the relationships we have in the body of

Christ, but to come away from the system - the spirit of Babylon that rules those organisations.

In the seventeenth chapter of John Jesus prays about the unity of the body of Christ:

I pray that they will all be one, just as you and I are one—as you are in me, Father, and I am in you. And may they be in us so that the world will believe you sent me.
John 17:21.

Our disunity not only harms us but also dismays the Godhead who we are one with.

The purpose of our unity is so that the world might believe.

Can we be surprised that church is the source of so much scorn and mockery.

This has little to do with our beliefs and everything to do with the foolishness that church systems present.

We can learn much from a well known verse of scripture:

For where two or three gather together as my followers, I am there among them."
Matthew 18:20.

We need not be afraid to remove ourselves from the larger group - there are an abundance of scriptures that speak about the preference of the Lord to use the small, the weak, the lesser, and the few.

We might take a closer look at what Jesus was saying in Matthew 18:20 above.

This verse is not by way of encouragement to support a small group but it is a declaration of power and purpose - the Lord is there, where two and three are together in unity, in a way that He is not in large church gatherings.

Where there are many people the Lord finds it difficult to make His voice heard - man will control the situation, normally with pre-planned services - the prompting of God's Spirit will not be an option even if the congregation have ears to hear Him.

But in a small related gathering of friends we will all have ears to hear Him and voices to speak what we hear.

The life of God is able to be shared with few people, in reality - we are able to grow and to mature as we share the life of the Spirit.

When we are gathered together on a relationship basis, we can be adaptable - to respond to what the Lord is saying to us in a way that is not possible in large gatherings that are led and manipulated by a few or one person.

Where there are a small number, we are able to build loving relationships.

There will be fluidity of movement between us, and other Christians we might not otherwise have known, when we are not suppressed by a church structure.

In a small gathering we will have the opportunity to become responsible for ourselves and for each other.

More importantly we will have the opportunity to hear and respond to the voice of God's Spirit when we are expecting to hear Him, rather than a voice from the leadership.

We are called to be inclusive rather than exclusive in our relationships.

We are born into God's Kingdom in order to live in unity with each other, not only with a select few who belong to our church or denomination.

We were born into the kingdom for freedom and not structure.

The *'ekklesia'* of God are not a people born into an organisation but a people born out of relationship - firstly a relationship with the Godhead and secondly with each other.

It is through relationships, hearing and responding to the Lord that we are able to grow - to become mature adults.

The life of the *'ekklesia'* is a life lived out of relationship with each other throughout the week - each day, and not simply a cloak that is to be worn on the day that church is open.

If we are truly living in relationship with each other we will be enjoying the company of each other regularly throughout the week and not simply meeting to support a service, an organisation or an event.

Our times together will be relaxed and enjoyable, sharing the Lord, whilst eating and drinking, walking or sharing a hobby.

Paul was writing with regards to the laws of Moses when he penned the following verse, but we too often fall into the same trap of living according to man's laws, or the laws of our local denomination, that the Galatians were guilty of.

So Christ has truly set us free. Now make sure that you stay free, and don't get tied up again in slavery to the law.
Galatians 5:1.

Jesus is with us when we are obedient to Him:

"So don't be afraid, little flock.

For it gives your Father great happiness to give you the Kingdom.
Luke 12:32.

To those who love Him, He is pleased to give us His kingdom.

Let us begin to shake off the chains of slavery to tradition and to the very many doctrines of religion.

There is no need to continue to delve into the sad situation within the church organisations that exist today.

Let us simply move on and leave those systems to their fate.

We may have read enough, but for any who wish to discover more it may be interesting to look into how and when, the people of the way, as Christians were widely known during the first centuries, became what they are now known as - church.

I believe the phrase, the people of the way, has a good sound to it.

It describes a people who have direction and a people who are rooted in Jesus, who is the Way, the Truth and the Life.

Jesus told him, "I am the way, the truth, and the life. No one can come to the Father except through me.
John 14:6.

We can see within the first four chapters of the book of Revelation how the people of the way were beginning to lose their way.

The letters that John was required to write to those people described some who were already becoming deceived.

There is no doubt that the seven letters in the book of Revelation are also addressed to us, today, but primarily the recipients were living during the latter days of the first century.

It was during that period that a hierarchy was also beginning to appear, Bishops had been appointed to rule over various areas, in contrast to the way that Jesus told us to be.

"Don't let anyone call you 'Rabbi,' for you have only one teacher, and all of you are equal as brothers and sisters.

And don't address anyone here on earth as 'Father,' for only God in heaven is your Father.

And don't let anyone call you 'Teacher,' for you have only one teacher, the Messiah.
Matthew 23:8-10.

I have discussed in previous books the New Testament understanding and application of the terms, leaders and elders, readers are welcome to discover a scriptural concept of these terms in those books

Suffice it to say they are not the equivalent of the manner in which the church applies them today - we will let the words of Jesus above speak for themselves.

We can see from reading the Acts of the Apostles and the letters that were written to the Christians in other places, that whilst the initial followers of Jesus died, mostly as martyrs, being executed by the Roman government, the disciples of those followers continued to teach and to discipline the thousands of Christians who had come into the kingdom.
Despite being persecuted, fed to wild beasts and killed for their efforts, the good news of the kingdom was becoming established on earth and Christians were becoming widespread and known throughout the world for the miracles that followed them and their way of life.

However, we can also see from those same letters that there were people coming into the gatherings of believers who were bringing in various false doctrines and deviations that were not as Jesus had taught.

On the one hand the kingdom was growing, had come to the notice of the Roman governments and was perceived as being a threat to the Roman empire, and on the other hand there were already false doctrines and misunderstandings beginning to be taught.

We can see from the later writings from the second, third and fourth generation of Christians how disagreements regarding the faith were beginning to create difficulties and a disunity among them.

It was the Emperor Constantine who finally plunged the people of the way into complete darkness by introducing various laws that prohibited the meeting of Christians in any place other than designated church buildings.

He passed laws prohibiting the feast days and celebrations that were widely celebrated, and instituted a hierarchy of priests and lay preachers, among many other prohibitive laws that made life harsh for the followers of Jesus.

The people of the way were no longer permitted to minister to each other, no longer allowed to meet in their homes, no longer allowed to keep passover or to pray outside of the temple-like buildings that Constantine had built.

Christians were forced to worship on one day only - a saturday, at a service that was prescribed and administered by priests in much the same way as the priests of the various gods and cults in the Roman world worshipped, in their pagan temples.

By introducing these, and other, measures throughout the Roman kingdom, Constantine was able to establish the counterfeit religion that was continued by the Roman Catholic church for centuries, and has continued in very much the same form and system, with some few variations, today.

There have been some changes as different revelations of truth have been received by those who have been faithful and have moved forward with God, only for those same faithful movements to be left behind when a following move of God came.

This has continued, leaving an array of different denominations, all of whom believe they are still living in the will of God.

The Lord moves on and if we are not aware of that moving we will inevitably be left behind, still living in an old revelation, while others move forward with the new.

It is good that there has been some forward movement with the children of God over the centuries, it is clear that there are some who have ears to hear and it also gives us encouragement that the Lord cares about those who are his.

We are not left alone.

It is also clear that there has been a constant call for those who are listening to come out of the dead and dying previous moves of God.

It is sad that there have been so many who have not been willing to move forward with Him and have been left behind.

It has been interesting to see how church has reacted to the recent laws, forbidding the gathering in buildings whilst the Covid - 19 pandemic has been at it's most virulent.

Far from welcoming the release from the very buildings and counterfeit religion that Constantine forced the people of the way into nearly two thousand years previously, there has rather been a great outcry that their freedoms are being denied.

It seems that church is no longer able to live as the 'ekklesia'.

But those who are not listening now will soon hear another voice stirring them.

The Lord is again talking to us, in these last days.

We are leaving the church age behind and moving into the age of kingdom.

In truth, we have always been living in the age of kingdom, but the Lord is calling us into an awareness now of all that kingdom is.

It is becoming clear that church is not kingdom.

The ways of church are contrary to the ways of God's kingdom.

The Lord has continually been calling us to come out of her.

Whilst we have made faltering steps of obedience - we have moved forward in stages into different revelations, we have been slow in hearing that call to move out of her completely and into the ways of kingdom life.

The picture is becoming clear now - we are not church - we are *'ekklesia'* - we are becoming a people who live in His kingdom.

Heaven is coming - Jesus is returning - His kingdom is becoming established on earth.

Baptism:

I have spoken with many who deny the teachings of scripture, by claiming that baptism is not necessary for becoming a Christain.

I have been amazed that this teaching often comes from theological colleges and so to the pulpits of those who have taken upon themselves the responsibility of leading.

I must make it clear from the beginning here, that by using the word baptism I am not describing a christening, or the sprinkling of a child at birth.

There can be no useful purpose served by this act which is no more than a superstitious gesture.

The act of christening a child at birth was introduced by the church in mediaeval times in the belief that if a child were baptised it might enter Heaven if it were to die early.

It was purported to be an indication that the child had joined the church and was therefore in some way made holy by that act.

In truth it is no more than a superstitious ritual.

Unless we make a decision for Jesus ourselves there is no benefit for us in another making that decision for us, or by coercing us to make that decision.

We can be assured that the Lord knows how to look after the ones who die before they are able to make a decision for Jesus.

It would be useful here to look at some verses we have previously looked at and some others.

For the writer of the letter to the Hebrew Christians, baptism was one of the foundation stones of the Christian faith.

So let us stop going over the basic teachings about Christ again and again.

Let us go on instead and become mature in our understanding.

Surely we don't need to start again with the fundamental importance of repenting from evil deeds and placing our faith in God.

You don't need further instruction about baptisms, the laying on of hands, the resurrection of the dead, and eternal judgement.
Hebrews 6:1-2

The writer of the letter to the Hebrews was sure that there was no need to keep going over the teaching about baptism - this was basic stuff.

Apparently, for modern teachers in the church, it isn't so basic.

Jesus explained that this was the case when He spoke to Nicodemus:

Jesus replied, "I assure you, no one can enter the Kingdom of God without being born of water and the Spirit.
John 3:5.

New believers coming into God's kingdom ought to be given instruction with regards to baptism and the foundations of the faith from the very beginning, but we still hear the question: is baptism for me?

Following our repentance and declaration of faith in Jesus, the next step for us is baptism.

Peter declared this to be the case on the day of Pentecost - the day that God's Spirit came to live with us.

Peter's words pierced their hearts, and they said to him and to the other apostles, "Brothers, what should we do?"

Peter replied, *"Each of you must repent of your sins and turn to God, and be baptised in the name of Jesus Christ for the forgiveness of your sins.*

Then you will receive the gift of the Holy Spirit. This promise is to you, to your children, and to those far away—all who have been called by the Lord our God."
Acts of the Apostles 2:37-39.

There are some who believe that baptism in water is simply a symbolic act that has no significance or has any effect in our lives.

Let's see how incorrect this doctrine is:

In the book of Acts we can read a short, but very pertinent, story about a group of people that Paul came across one day:

While Apollos was in Corinth, Paul travelled through the interior regions until he reached Ephesus, on the coast, where he found several believers.

"Did you receive the Holy Spirit when you believed?" he asked them.
"No," they replied, "we haven't even heard that there is a Holy Spirit."
"Then what baptism did you experience?" he asked.

And they replied, "The baptism of John."

Paul said, "John's baptism called for repentance from sin.
But John himself told the people to believe in the one who would come later, meaning Jesus."
As soon as they heard this, they were baptised in the name of the Lord Jesus.

Then when Paul laid his hands on them, the Holy Spirit came on them, and they spoke in other tongues and prophesied.
There were about twelve men in all.
Acts of the Apostles 19:1-7.

It is clear from our story that Paul noticed that these followers were different to others who had been born again and he asked a question in order to discover why that was.

It transpired that these followers hadn't heard of Jesus, their baptism had been one of repentance by John the baptist.

They had not been baptised into new life, by faith in Jesus but into John the baptist's baptism of repentance.

Paul explained to them what Jesus had accomplished for them by dying in our place - He took the death that we were due, and was raised again from death in order to show that He had overcome the consequences of sin, and then immediately baptised them into Jesus, and then God's Spirit filled them all.

Paul realised, from the first, that something was missing in these believers' lives.

They had been baptised in water by John the baptist but Paul recognised that they were no different to others living in the world.

We have probably come across this amongst church goers, and others who claim to have been born again, ourselves.

We, who have been truly born again are able to identify those who do not know Jesus by their speech and actions.

As soon as the followers that Paul had met understood what Jesus had accomplished and had been baptised in water, God's Spirit filled them.

Only Baptism into Jesus enables the Spirit to come, which initiates change in us.

Humans can reproduce human life, but God's Spirit gives birth to spiritual life.
John 3:6.

Baptism brings a relationship with Father; It is only through our baptism that we can become sons and daughters of God.

One day Jesus came from Nazareth in Galilee, and John baptised him in the Jordan River.

As Jesus came up out of the water, he saw the heavens splitting apart and the Holy Spirit descending on him like a dove.
Mark 1:9-10.

Jesus, who was sinless, asked to be baptised in order to fulfil all righteousness.

It is through baptism that we are able to become righteous - unless we are baptised into Jesus we remain in our unrighteousness.

Then Jesus came from Galilee to John at the Jordan [River], to be baptised by him.

But John tried to prevent Him [vigorously protesting], saying, "It is I who need to be baptised by You, and do You come to me?"

But Jesus replied to him, "Permit it just now; for this is the fitting way for us to fulfil all righteousness." Then John permitted [it and baptised] Him.
Matthew 3:13-15.(amp).

Unless we become baptised we remain outside of the body of Christ - we can only become one body through baptism.

Some of us are Jews, some are Gentiles, some are slaves, and some are free.

But we have all been baptised into one body by one Spirit, and we all share the same Spirit.
1 Corinthians 12:13.

Repentance and then Baptism initiates - begins the process of having our minds renewed.

There is one Lord, one faith, one baptism, throw off your old sinful nature and your former way of life, which is corrupted by lust and deception.

Instead, let the Spirit renew your thoughts and attitudes.

Put on your new nature, created to be like God—truly righteous and holy.
Ephesians 4:5, 22-24.

When our thoughts are brought into line with God's thoughts, our words and actions also change - Jesus begins to be revealed in us.

Baptism is one of the first steps of faith which, in turn, leads to further steps of faith.

We live by faith. If we don't take a first step there will be no other steps.

It is only by faith that we become overcomers.

Therefore baptism leads to overcoming - it leads us into victory.

When we are baptised we enter the kingdom through Jesus - Jesus is the doorway, the access to Father.

Jesus told him, "I am the way, the truth, and the life. No one can come to the Father except through me.
John 14:6.

Jesus is the way. Jesus is the truth. Jesus is the life.

Baptism brings about changes in our life.

When we live in satan's kingdom of death we are unable to prevent ourselves from doing wrong, in our thoughts and activities.

When we choose Jesus, we make the decision to move from one kingdom; the kingdom of satan, into God's kingdom - the kingdom of life.

We repent of our old life of sin - we say sorry and we realise that Jesus has opened a way by which we can be brought back into life with Father.

Jesus died so that we can be saved from our old way of life.

Then we decide to move from slavery to a life of sin, into a life of slavery to Jesus.

When we enter the water of baptism our old life of sin is washed away, it goes forever.

Or have you forgotten that when we were joined with Christ Jesus in baptism, we joined him in his death?

For we died and were buried with Christ by baptism.

And just as Christ was raised from the dead by the glorious power of the Father, now we also may live new lives.
Romans 6:3-4.

For you were buried with Christ when you were baptised. And with him you were raised to new life because you trusted the mighty power of God, who raised Christ from the dead.
Colossians 2:12.

Baptism in water is a time when we are buried - our old self dies and we take on a new life - the life of Jesus.

Our old man is crucified with Jesus - we are buried with Him in baptism.

When we take a serious look at scripture we find that baptism is crucial to moving into and growing in the kingdom.

When we rise up out of the water we are born again into a new family - God's family.

But to all who believed him and accepted him, he gave the right to become children of God.

They are reborn—not with a physical birth resulting from human passion or plan, but a birth that comes from God. John 1:13.

Through baptism we become one with Father, Son and with Spirit.

I pray that they will all be one, just as you and I are one—as you are in me, Father, and I am in you. And may they be in us so that the world will believe you sent me.

"I have given them the glory you gave me, so they may be one as we are one.

I am in them and you are in me. May they experience such perfect unity that the world will know that you sent me and that you love them as much as you love me. John 17:21-23.

We enter the waters of baptism in faith because we love Him and because we trust that what Jesus tells us is true - He will never let us down.

Jesus replied, "All who love me will do what I say.

My Father will love them, and we will come and make our home with each of them.
John 14:23.

Baptism enables us to live for Jesus.

Without baptism we remain slaves to sin.

Many who have been taught that baptism has no use for them continue to live with the consequences of sin in their lives - they have no faith in what Jesus requires of us, in order for us to enter into His kingdom and so they remain with their feet firmly embedded still in rebellion to God, in the kingdom of the enemy.

We can read another instance of Baptism in scripture, where God sovereignly decided to baptise some Gentiles in His Spirit to show Peter and his friends that He does not discriminate between Jew and Gentile.

Even as Peter was saying these things, the Holy Spirit fell upon all who were listening to the message.

The Jewish believers who came with Peter were amazed that the gift of the Holy Spirit had been poured out on the Gentiles, too.

For they heard them speaking in other tongues and praising God.

Then Peter asked, "Can anyone object to their being baptised, now that they have received the Holy Spirit just as we did?"
Acts of the Apostles 10:44-47.

The Lord told Peter to go and speak to some Gentiles about Jesus.

Peter wasn't keen to mix with Gentiles, he was a devout Jew, but despite his feelings he went to talk to them anyway.

It must have been quite a culture shock for Peter to enter the house of a Gentile.

Having heard what Peter had to say, the Gentiles were keen to repent and to change their ways, and so Father, realising that Peter would be reticent to let these unclean Gentiles into the kingdom, sovereignly baptised them in His Spirit - they were immersed in God's Spirit.

Peter quickly realised what had occurred and that he must therefore baptise them in water.

If God takes baptism seriously, we ought to as well.

There can be no argument left against the necessity to be baptised in water.

It is not necessary to be qualified to baptise another.

The only qualification we need is to be acting out of obedience to Father.

A mature Christian would be preferable, to give advice and guidance, but not essential.

The act of baptism is a union between the Godhead and the person being baptised.

There is also a union with us and the whole family of God, throughout the ages.

Baptism is a momentous event in a believer's life; a cause of great joy and celebration.

Therefore it is hoped that there will be others to share in the occasion, but it is not necessary.

The Godhead and angels will be present.

Baptism in Spirit is also widely misunderstood.

We have touched briefly on the baptism of God's Spirit but it would be wise to enlarge upon what we already know.

For a subject that can be ignored or rejected, among certain groups, there are plenty of scriptures that refer to it.

I believe that peer pressure amongst certain denominational groups is often the cause of this rejection.

If one influential member of a group has not experienced the baptism of God's Spirit then it is an easy task to persuade others that there is no necessity.

Where there is no faith for a spiritual aspect of God there will be no fruit of the Spirit in activity there.

The baptism of God's Spirit can also be referred to as the gift of God's Spirit - God's Spirit is a gift.

Peter replied, "Each of you must repent of your sins and turn to God, and be baptised in the name of Jesus Christ for the forgiveness of your sins.

Then you will receive the gift of the Holy Spirit.
Acts of the Apostles 2:38.

Repentance, or a desire to change, and faith in Jesus, will be followed by our baptism into Jesus, in water.

Our faith and obedience to Him will prompt Father to baptise us - to immerse us, in His Spirit.

It is the act of being immersed in God's Spirit that is the confirmation that we have been welcomed into His family.

God is Spirit and therefore if we are to be transformed into His likeness, we too must be thoroughly immersed in Him.

But whenever someone turns to the Lord, the veil is taken away.

For the Lord is the Spirit, and wherever the Spirit of the Lord is, there is freedom.

So all of us who have had that veil removed can see and reflect the glory of the Lord.
And the Lord—who is the Spirit—makes us more and more like him as we are changed into his glorious image.
2 Corinthians 3:16-18.

We can readily understand the implications if we are not immersed in Him.

Jesus replied, "I assure you, no one can enter the Kingdom of God without being born of water and the Spirit.
John 3:5.

Jesus told His disciples that they would be baptised in His Spirit and that it would be necessary for them to be so, in order to receive His power.

John baptised with water, but in just a few days you will be baptised with the Holy Spirit."

But you will receive power when the Holy Spirit comes upon you.

And you will be my witnesses, telling people about me everywhere—in Jerusalem, throughout Judea, in Samaria, and to the ends of the earth."
Acts of the Apostles 1:7-8

Baptism in God's Spirit enables a witness - the declaration of Jesus to the world, which is expressed by the fact that He reveals Himself through us.

It is only through the baptism in God's Spirit that we can become one with Him and with each other.

Some of us are Jews, some are Gentiles, some are slaves, and some are free.

But we have all been baptised into one body by one Spirit, and we all share the same Spirit.
1 Corinthians 12:13.

John the baptist spoke of Jesus, who would baptise us with His spirit.

"I baptise with water those who repent of their sins and turn to God.

*But someone is coming soon who is greater than I am—
so much greater that I'm not worthy even to be his slave
and carry his sandals.*

*He will baptise you with the Holy Spirit and with fire.
Matthew 3:11.*

Baptism in God's Spirit is not necessarily a single event.

There was a time of fierce persecution for the followers of Jesus, Peter and John were brought before the courts and cautioned.

As a result of this, the followers came together and prayed about the situation they were in - they were terrified.

It is interesting to note that these followers had already been baptised in God's Spirit at Pentecost.

But the scriptures tell us that after some prayer, they were filled again:

After this prayer, the meeting place shook, and they were all filled with the Holy Spirit.

*Then they preached the word of God with boldness.
Acts of the Apostles 4:31.*

There is no limit to God's baptism with us.

There will be times when we will be moving into a new sphere of authority on the earth, and the Lord will baptise us again with Himself in order to bring a fresh depth of power.

As we move forward with Him there will be continual immersings.

It is sobering to realise that without God's Spirit we do not belong to Him at all.

But you are not controlled by your sinful nature.
You are controlled by the Spirit if you have the Spirit of God living in you.

(And remember that those who do not have the Spirit of Christ living in them do not belong to him at all.)
Romans 8:9.

We can understand from these scriptures that Father wants us to be baptised in His Spirit.

We can see that unless we are baptised in water and in Spirit we cannot enter God's kingdom.

When we are born again through baptism we become a new creation - a Spirit filled creation.

This means that anyone who belongs to Christ has become a new person. The old life is gone; a new life has begun!

2 Corinthians 5:17.

There are a plethora of scriptures that teach about baptism.

It is essential for us to be baptised in Spirit to gain entry to God's kingdom.

God is Spirit. The only way that we can be one with Him is for us also to become Spirit.

Knowing that Father wants us to be baptised in Spirit enables us to have faith that He will do just that if we ask Him to.

Through baptism in His Spirit God gives us spiritual gifts.

Some of these are mentioned in a letter that Paul wrote to the Corinthians:

A spiritual gift is given to each of us so we can help each other.
To one person the Spirit gives the ability to give wise advice; to another the same Spirit gives a message of special knowledge.

The same Spirit gives great faith to another, and to someone else the one Spirit gives the gift of healing.

He gives one person the power to perform miracles, and another the ability to prophesy.
He gives someone else the ability to discern whether a message is from the Spirit of God or from another spirit.

Still another person is given the ability to speak in unknown languages, while another is given the ability to interpret what is being said.

It is the one and only Spirit who distributes all these gifts. He alone decides which gift each person should have.
1 Corinthians 12:7-11.

Our Spiritual gifts have a dual purpose:

To encourage and build each other, and ourselves up, and to defeat the enemy - to pull down demonic strongholds.

The phrase, praying in the Spirit, is another way of talking about praying in tongues.

When we pray in tongues we are effectively having a Spirit conversation with Father.

Our Spirit, the Spirit that is now living with us, speaks to Father in words or sounds that we don't understand with our natural mind.

For if you have the ability to speak in tongues, you will be talking only to God, since people won't be able to understand you.
You will be speaking by the power of the Spirit, but it will all be mysterious.
1 Corinthians 14:2.

The language is unintelligible for us but as we speak in tongues, often the meaning becomes clear to us.

This is described as the interpretation of tongues.

When we are alone with Father speaking in tongues, the interpretation isn't always necessary because our Spirit understands the words that we speak.

When we are speaking in tongues with others present then interpretation becomes more necessary so that we can all understand what Father is saying to us.

He gives one person the power to perform miracles, and another the ability to prophesy.

He gives someone else the ability to discern whether a message is from the Spirit of God or from another spirit.

Still another person is given the ability to speak in unknown languages, while another is given the ability to interpret what is being said.
1 Corinthians 12:10.

We will find that singing in tongues is also useful as it releases praise and worship to God that is led by the Spirit within us.

Revelation and prophecy, words of wisdom and knowledge, and other gifts often come when, or after tongues are present.

The use of tongues releases a spiritual aspect into our lives when we are with Father, and also when we are with others.

Jesus is able to reveal Himself to us, and others, as we operate in the Spirit realm in this way.

The use of tongues releases us in prayer.

And the Holy Spirit helps us in our weakness. For example, we don't know what God wants us to pray for.

But the Holy Spirit prays for us with groanings that cannot be expressed in words.

And the Father who knows all hearts knows what the Spirit is saying, for the Spirit pleads for us believers in harmony with God's own will.
Romans 8:26-27.

When Spirit filled people come together there are many Spiritual gifts that we can all benefit from as we share the life of God with each other.

Well, my brothers and sisters, let's summarise.

When you meet together, one will sing, another will teach, another will tell some special revelation God has given, one will speak in tongues, and another will interpret what is said.

But everything that is done must strengthen all of you.

No more than two or three should speak in tongues. They must speak one at a time, and someone must interpret what they say.

But if no one is present who can interpret, they must be silent in your church meeting and speak in tongues to God privately.
Let two or three people prophesy, and let the others evaluate what is said.

But if someone is prophesying and another person receives a revelation from the Lord, the one who is speaking must stop. In this way, all who prophesy will have a turn to speak, one after the other, so that everyone will learn and be encouraged.

Remember that people who prophesy are in control of their spirit and can take turns.
1 Corinthians 14:26-32.

The Spirit and our Spiritual gifts remain with us - we are one with Spirit, so that we are able to live in the fullness of God whether we are alone or with others.

We will need to practice our gifts.

This is why I remind you to fan into flames the spiritual gift God gave you when I laid my hands on you.
2 Timothy 1:6.

It is sometimes necessary for hands to be laid upon a person for God's Spirit to come.

This might be because the enemy does not want to release the person being baptised, but there can be other reasons.

When the apostles in Jerusalem heard that the people of Samaria had accepted God's message, they sent Peter and John there.

As soon as they arrived, they prayed for these new believers to receive the Holy Spirit.

The Holy Spirit had not yet come upon any of them, for they had only been baptised in the name of the Lord Jesus.

Then Peter and John laid their hands upon these believers, and they received the Holy Spirit.
Acts of the Apostles 8:14-17.

When a Christian's hands are used they link God, who is Spirit, with whoever the hands are laid upon.

At a person's baptism it will be usual for others gathered to prophesy into the newly baptised person's life.

Spiritual gifts are often imparted by the laying on of hands at baptism, according to the faith and maturity of the believers gathered.

This is something that Timothy experienced.

Do not neglect the spiritual gift you received through the prophecy spoken over you when the elders of the church laid their hands on you.
1 Timothy 4:14.

Being baptised opens the way for our mind to be renewed.

Don't copy the behaviour and customs of this world, but let God transform you into a new person by changing the way you think.

Then you will learn to know God's will for you, which is good and pleasing and perfect.
Romans 12:2.

What can we do if we have previously not understood baptism or have not yet received God's Spirit?

If we have not received baptism we need to talk to someone who has been born into God's kingdom, about becoming baptised.

This will not necessarily be a church member or a leader, as we have discovered previously, but a person who knows Jesus.

There is a contact address at the end of this book for anyone who would like more information and advice.

The only person who I am aware of, who was not baptised, and promised a place in God's eternity in scripture, is the thief on the cross.

There was neither the opportunity or the necessity for him to be baptised, as he was not going to face the trials of life that others do.

Baptism is essential if we are to overcome the enemy who will attempt to destroy us.

As we have seen earlier, scripture advises us that we receive power when we are baptised.

We become one with the Godhead and with others in the new family when we are baptised - unless we become one we will die spiritually for lack of spiritual food.

It is necessary that we become baptised in water which is a step of faith leading us into the new kingdom.

There are no occasions that I am aware of, where a person has immersed themselves in water for baptism.

Baptism is a grand occasion and I believe should be enjoyed with those we will be sharing the life of Jesus with.

However, if it is not possible to share with others, I can see no reason why water baptism can not be shared with Father and the angels.

There is normally at least one other to immerse the new believer in the name of the Father and the Son and the Spirit.

There is no other name by which we can be saved.

There is salvation in no one else! God has given no other name under heaven by which we must be saved."
Acts of the Apostles 4:12.

When we are immersed in water we become one with the Godhead.

At the time of Pentecost the disciples were all together when they were baptised in God's Spirit.

Very soon after the disciples were baptised, there were about three thousand people who were also baptised together - what a party that must have been.

I know of many who have been alone when God has immersed them in Spirit.

It is an occasion that can be enjoyed with Father in isolation.

I believe that these occasions work far better when God's family is present, after all, we are born into a shared unity and not born to live in isolation.

From my own experience, I was not aware that there was a baptism in God's Spirit at the time I was immersed in Him.

I had been baptised with water in obedience, not knowing too much of what the occasion was about, and told that was the end of the matter - I was on the way to Heaven and left to manage that future.

It wasn't until some months later that I found myself in bed one evening with a desire to praise Jesus, who had died for me, that I became immersed in His Spirit and began speaking words that I didn't understand.

I only knew that they were sounds of thanks and praise and that I was communicating with my Father.

It was sometime later that I learnt about being baptised in Spirit and realised that was what had happened.

We can appreciate that sometimes Father works sovereignly and takes matters into his own hands - He is allowed to do that - we belong to Him.

I am sure that the disciples weren't fully aware of what was going to occur at the time of Passover, when the Spirit descended upon them.

It wasn't until afterwards that Peter was able to explain what had happened.

Then Peter stepped forward with the eleven other apostles and shouted to the crowd, "Listen carefully, all of you, fellow Jews and residents of Jerusalem!

Make no mistake about this.

These people are not drunk, as some of you are assuming.
Nine o'clock in the morning is much too early for that.

No, what you see was predicted long ago by the prophet Joel:

'In the last days,' God says, 'I will pour out my Spirit upon all people.
Your sons and daughters will prophesy.

Your young men will see visions, and your old men will dream dreams.

In those days I will pour out my Spirit even on my servants—men and women alike— and they will prophesy.
Acts of the Apostles 2:14-18.

In some ways it is better for us not to be prepared for what Father wants to do with us.

We can limit Him by our expectations, and so for me to write down what to expect when we are baptised in water and in His Spirit, would be wrong as He is sovereign and will do with us whatever He chooses - we can be sure that it will be the best experience ever, if He is involved.

Our only responsibility is to be obedient and to live in faith knowing that He will always fill us with His love.

Summing up.

So, what can we say about our general understanding of scripture?

Can we be confident that what we read in our Bibles is correct?

Paul wrote to Timothy with regards to the scriptures:

All Scripture is inspired by God and is useful to teach us what is true and to make us realise what is wrong in our lives.
It corrects us when we are wrong and teaches us to do what is right.

God uses it to prepare and equip his people to do every good work.
2 Timothy 3:16-17.

We can be sure that the scriptures are inspired by God, as Paul suggested that they are.

We can also be confident that the Bible is useful to us for teaching and correction.

Without the Bible we would have no knowledge of many great and wonderful works of God or of His dealings with mankind.

I have known of many who have been brought to a knowledge of Jesus simply by reading a Bible.

The Bible reveals Jesus to us.

However, we must not make the mistake of assuming that the Bible has been correctly translated for us in every instance, or that the Bible is the infallible word of God.

The Bible that we read, are not the scriptures that Paul and others refer to, but are a translation of scriptures that were written many hundreds of years ago in many different, known, and now unknown, languages.

The Bible is a book.

It is Jesus who is the word of God.

The Bible is a book that has the words of God and the manner in which God has interacted with His creation, faithfully copied into it.

In the beginning the Word already existed. The Word was with God, and the Word was God.
He existed in the beginning with God.

God created everything through him, and nothing was created except through him.

The Word gave life to everything that was created, and his life brought light to everyone.
John 1:1-4.

It is through the word of God - who is Jesus, that we obtain direction, truth and life, - He is the way, the truth and the life.

We are treading on very thin ice when we declare emphatically, something that we have not necessarily heard, first hand from the word, who is Jesus.

We have discovered that translators are fallible, they make mistakes, as we all do at times.

Only God knows the beginning from the end.

What we can say is that He knows our weaknesses and will direct us into eternity in ways that only He will know.

Our responsibility is to develop listening ears so that we can hear when He says - 'go this way', or 'go that way'.

Your own ears will hear him.
Right behind you a voice will say, "This is the way you should go," whether to the right or to the left.
Isaiah 30:21.

Until we learn to hear His words, that are guidance for us, we will continue to behave like dumb animals, following the herd, or like sheep being led away from the shepherd into the lair of ravenous wolves.

For the leaders of my people— the Lord's watchmen, his shepherds— are blind and ignorant.
They are like silent watchdogs that give no warning when danger comes.
They love to lie around, sleeping and dreaming.

Like greedy dogs, they are never satisfied.
They are ignorant shepherds, all following their own path and intent on personal gain.
Isaiah 56:10-1.

As we can readily appreciate there is a need at this time to listen to what God's Spirit is saying to each one of us.

For far too long we have been hesitant, stumbling along making small adjustments here and there, without ever fully entering into His presence in the way we are born to.

To live in God's kingdom with Him is our inheritance.

It was a hard won victory that was accomplished by Jesus on our behalf.

It cost Him His life.

We must not allow the thief - the deceiver, to rob us of what has been given to us.

Those of us with ears to hear are leaving the church age behind and are entering into the kingdom age that is now upon us.

Will you follow the shepherd into rich, green pastures or wait behind for the herd, who may not hear the voice that you have heard.

Paul wasn't simply painting a rosy picture for us when he wrote these words:

For he raised us from the dead along with Christ and seated us with him in the heavenly realms because we are united with Christ Jesus.
Ephesians 2:6.

Paul was speaking from a personal experience of the reality that each one of us have been brought into.

There are always further questions and enquiries to be made in the Christian life – everything is new!

There is always something to discover – something new to share with others.

Please feel free to email me if you have any questions, or would like to talk about this book.

To contact Tim - the author:
email: warwickhouse@mail.com

Tim has also written:

Journey Into Life:

What did Jesus really preach about when He was on earth?
Within "A Journey into Life" we discover the joy of travelling to a new place.

Tim has set our search for God's kingdom in the form of a journey to a new land.

Once inside the new land we begin a journey of discovery – everything is new.

Did Jesus teach that His kingdom is within our grasp?
Is this a land – A kingdom that we can live in now – in our own lifetime?

The answer is yes!

Some Adjustments Required?:

We live our lives from day to day carrying out regular routines and rituals often without thinking about what we do and what we say and why.

We take for granted that the things that we have done and said and even for centuries past must be correct because that is simply the way things are.

Tim has taken some of the many misunderstood concepts in the Christian life that we have, for so long, taken for granted and brought correction and redirection.

God is doing a new thing in this season and those who want to follow His direction need to hear Him.

A Time To Consider:

A Time to consider was written at a time when several friends and friends of friends had been taken Ill by potentially life threatening illnesses.

When this happens to us out of the blue it is naturally a shocking discovery to realise that we aren't going to live on this earth, in this body, forever.

It is however a reality that we all need to take into consideration.

Any of us may be taken away at any time.
Our life on earth is a very short period when we consider eternity.

Let us get involved with eternity now - we may not get another opportunity to do so.

The Shaking:

We live in a changing era.
God is moving and the earth is being shaken.
The church age is passing.
God's kingdom age is upon us.
How do the times that we live fit with God's plan for us in eternity?
Has our own past affected our present and will it affect our future?
Can we make an impact in our time?

Our Foundations:

Many of us have missed out on vital foundational truths in our walk with the Lord.
Consequently we tend to wander around unaware that we may be missing out on the good things that Father has planned for us, unsure of where we should be or what our purpose is here on earth.
As we look into "Our Foundations" some much needed clarity and understanding will be gleaned for our benefit and for that of the emerging kingdom.

Genesis part one:

There are many apparent mysteries for us to uncover when reading the book of Genesis.

In Genesis part one we attempt to uncover and give an answer to some of these mysteries.

We also invite the reader to consider the text for themselves and to appreciate that the Lord is wanting us to open up a discussion with Him.

Genesis part two:

In Genesis part two we continue to look at the line of progression that began with Adam and will continue to the birth of Jesus.

Noah has journeyed into a new era. Life has continued as the Lord promised.

Abraham, the man of faith and the father of all who choose to trust in Jesus, is born.

The nations begin to emerge from the mists.

Genesis part three:

Genesis part three brings us to the birth of Isaac who is a type of Jesus.

From Isaac, through Jacob, to Joseph and into the land of Egypt we can journey with the patriarchs and the children of the man who becomes Israel.

The Lord is bringing His plan of redemption to pass.

The End Times - for non Christians.

The end times for non Christians spells out, in a relatively short book, the times that we are living in now and the part that non Christians have to play at the end of this age.

Entering Eternity Today.

Do we go to Heaven when we die?

For over two thousand years there has been some considerable misunderstanding and confusion with regards to God's kingdom.

Where it is taught, the question is inevitably raised, what is God's kingdom?
Is it a place we go to when we die?

Will we be taken there one day?
The answer to that one is a definite, no.

The enemy has introduced much incorrect teaching into church circles in order to ensure that his kingdom remains.

When we uncover the truth of this deception and learn to live in God's promises he will flee like never before and the world will encounter a harvest unlike any other.

The Thief.

The basic beliefs and understandings of Christians are grounded in the interpretation of the scriptures that have been carried out by well meaning theologians.

But what happens to those basic foundations of truth when we discover that perhaps not all of those translations have been well made?

How great a part has the enemy of our faith played in the interpretation and representation of the scriptures that we read everyday in our Bibles?

We may find that we are living at a time when our understanding of scripture requires some adjustment if we are to enter into all that Father has in store for us.

Other recommended publications of related interest:

By John J Sweetman

Paperback and EBooks:

Establishing the kingdom series:

The Book of Joshua
The Book of Judges
The Book of Ruth
The Book of 1 Samuel
The Book of 2 Samuel
The Book of 1 Corinthians
The Book of 2 Corinthians
The Book of Galatians
The Book of Revelations
The Book of Romans
The Book of Hebrews
The Emerging kingdom

Babylon or Jerusalem – your choice

by Fiona Sweetman

Paperback and EBook
Taste the Colour Smell the Number

Printed in Great Britain
by Amazon